751.4
T
01

D0479715

JOY *to the* WORLD

Painting ──
HOLIDAY HEIRLOOMS

DATE DUE			

PRINTED IN U.S.A.

John Gutcher

NORTH LIGHT BOOKS
CINCINNATI, OHIO
www.artistsnetwork.com

CARSON CITY LIBRARY

about the author

JOHN GUTCHER IS ONE OF THE MOST RECOGNIZED AND POPULAR ARTISTS AND TEACHERS in the decorative painting field. John has appeared as guest artist on the TV series *Home Decorating Workshop* and on the PBS series *Perfect Palette*. He has written three project books and has been published in all the decorative painting magazines, including *Decorative Artist's Workbook*. In addition to teaching weekly oil and acrylic classes in his hometown of Tampa, Florida, John travel-teaches painting workshops to art organizations and at conventions throughout North America. His paintings have won numerous national, state and local awards, and his portraits hang in private collections in the U.S. and Canada.

JOY TO THE WORLD: PAINTING HOLIDAY HEIRLOOMS. Copyright © 2001 by John Gutcher. Manufactured in China. All rights reserved. The patterns and drawings in this book are for the personal use of the decorative painter. By permission of the author and publisher, they may be either hand-traced or photocopied to make single copies, but under no circumstances may they be resold or republished. It is permissible for the purchaser to paint the designs contained herein and sell them at fairs, bazaars and craft shows. No other part of this book may be reproduced in any form or by any electronic or mechanical means including information storage and retrieval systems without permission in writing from the publisher, except by a reviewer, who may quote brief passages in a review. Published by North Light Books, an imprint of F&W Publications, Inc., 1507 Dana Avenue, Cincinnati, Ohio 45207. (800) 289-0963. First edition.

Other fine North Light Books are available from your local bookstore, art supply store or direct from the publisher.

05 04 03 02 01   5 4 3 2 1

Library of Congress Cataloging-in-Publication Data

Gutcher, John.
   Joy to the world : painting holiday heirlooms / by John Gutcher.– 1st ed.
      p. cm.
   Includes index.
   ISBN 1-58180-105-X (pbk.: alk. paper)
   1. Christmas in art. 2. Santa Claus–Art. 3. Painting–Technique. I. Title
ND1430 .G88 2001
751.4–dc21   00-066992

Editor: Christine Doyle
Production Coordinator: Emily Gross
Designer: Andrea Short
Layout Artist: Lisa Holstein
Photographers: Christine Polomsky and Al Parrish
Photo Stylist: Jan Nickum

Metric Conversion Chart

to convert	to	multiply by
Inches	Centimeters	2.54
Centimeters	Inches	0.4
Feet	Centimeters	30.5
Centimeters	Feet	0.03
Yards	Meters	0.9
Meters	Yards	1.1
Sq. Inches	Sq. Centimeters	6.45
Sq. Centimeters	Sq. Inches	0.16
Sq. Feet	Sq. Meters	0.09
Sq. Meters	Sq. Feet	10.8
Sq. Yards	Sq. Meters	0.8
Sq. Meters	Sq. Yards	1.2
Pounds	Kilograms	0.45
Kilograms	Pounds	2.2
Ounces	Grams	28.4
Grams	Ounces	0.04

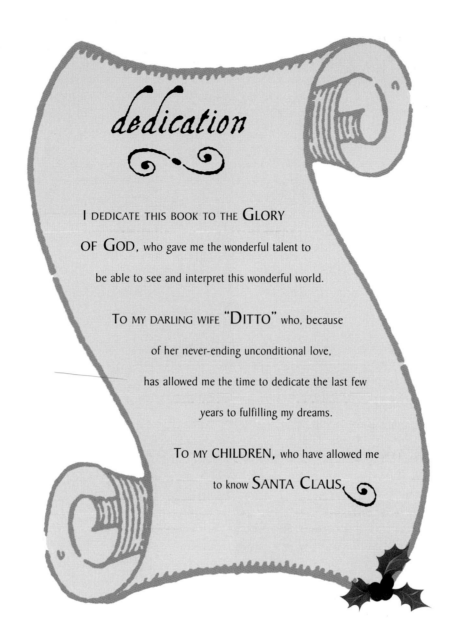

dedication

I DEDICATE THIS BOOK TO THE GLORY

OF GOD, who gave me the wonderful talent to

be able to see and interpret this wonderful world.

TO MY DARLING WIFE "DITTO" who, because

of her never-ending unconditional love,

has allowed me the time to dedicate the last few

years to fulfilling my dreams.

TO MY CHILDREN, who have allowed me

to know SANTA CLAUS.

acknowledgments

I would like to express my appreciation to my many instructors over the years

including JOHN SLOAN, FRANK COVINO, DANIEL GREEN and BEDE ANGLE. To the paint manufacturers

PLAID INTERNATIONAL, INC. and MARTIN/ F. WEBER CO. and to the ROYAL BRUSH MANUFACTURING

CO., for their faith in me that pushed me forward into an industry that I am forever grateful to be a part of.

INTRODUCTION

WHEN I THINK OF SANTA, I THINK OF HIM AS A REAL LIVE PERSON. He has rounded features, movement and vitality, warmth, even a twinkle in his eye. That's why when I paint Santa projects, they could actually be considered Santa portraits.

For this book I've created nine colorful projects to celebrate the holidays and most of them include Santa. The first Santa project is an introduction to painting a realistic face in acrylics; the last project teaches you how to paint a more detailed, museum-quality Santa portrait in oils. In between, the projects focus mainly on the many realistic views of the classic Santa Claus as well as angels, elves and Mrs. Claus. To make the Christmas settings complete, you'll also learn to paint additional holiday symbols such as children's toys, seasonal holly and pine needle foliage, a fireplace with glowing flames, a starry night, cardinals and tree boughs filled with snow.

Throughout this book the instructions and the techniques used are such that you can paint the projects in either acrylics or oils. I use a limited palette of mostly standard colors that can be found in both mediums, and my technique of applying a series of loose, overlapping brushstrokes mixed to multiple values can be done with either medium, too. (This technique is what gives these projects excitement and motion.)

Painting should be fun first and should always be an enjoyable experience. Use your imagination and paint these projects on the surfaces you enjoy. While many of the subjects could be painted on conventional canvas and framed for the living room wall, they're just as attractive as decorative subjects to enhance usable objects.

I hope that the many colorful subjects in this book will get you to start seeing Santa in a more realistic fashion and to pick up that brush and apply paint with "fun" in mind. And I hope the projects you paint will bring joy to the world!

—John Gutcher

CHAPTER ONE

Materials & Techniques

Basic Supplies

Following is a list of the basic supplies I have on hand for painting these projects and others as well.

1. Brushes: Have one set for your acrylic painting and one for oil painting.

2. Paints: Whether using acrylics or oils, I have a very simple palette of colors, then mix all the other values that I need.

3. Water brush basin: I use one by Royal Brush Co., series F, D-49.

4. Tack cloth

5. Sandpaper

6. Blue low-tack masking tape

7. Wood Sealer: I use J.W. etc. First-Step Wood Sealer.

8. Varnish: I use J.W. etc. Right-Step Clear Varnish. Whether you use matte or gloss on a project is your preference.

9. Palette: I suggest using the Sta-Wet Palette by Masterson, one for acrylics and one for oils. Or you may use a disposable paper palette pad for the oils. For my oil palette, I use one that

I've designed and had laminated. See the description on page 10.

10. Palette knife: My favorite is by Royal Brush Co., series X, P-16.

11. Graining tool: I recommend the series BB, LW117 Rubber Duplex Comb by Royal Brush.

12. Ruler

13. Sea sponge: I like the #2007 Sea Wool Sponge by Royal Brush Co.

14. Stylus

15. X-Acto knife or single-edge razor blades

16. 0.5mm mechanical pencil

17. Tracing paper

18. Gray and white transfer paper

• Paper towels

• Brush cleaner

What John Uses

Acrylics paints and mediums

Plaid FolkArt Artists' Pigment Acrylics • Plaid FolkArt Acrylics •
Martin/ F. Weber Co. Prima Acrylics • FolkArt Blending Gel Medium

Oil paints and medium

Martin/ F. Weber Co. Permalba and Prima Oil Paints •
Martin/ F. Weber Co. RapiDry Oil Medium •
Martin/ F. Weber Co. Odorless Turpenoid and Turpenoid Natural •
Containers with lids for oil painting medium and Turpenoid

Brushes

(one set for acrylics and another for oils)

Royal Fusion Brushes: series 3250 no. 2 and 3 round; series 3585 no. 2 script
liner; series 3130 no. 1, 6, 8, 10 and 12 flats; series 3170 no. 1, 6, 8 , 10
and 12 filberts • Royal Regis Bristle Brushes: series 405 no. 3 and 6 bristle fan •
Royal Supreme White Bristle Brushes: series 1AB no. 5 Bright;
series 1AT no. 5 filbert; series 1AR no. 1 round

Painting Techniques

The projects in this book are all painted in a rather loose style of painting that could be referred to as "painterly" in comparison to the usual smooth decorative painting style. I like to see my brushstrokes creating subtle value changes and textures. Many color values are mixed in the process to build solid form and construction. Then the details are added as the final touches. I compare my painting process to baking a cake or building a house. You first need a recipe or floor plan, then you add all the ingredients or the foundation to make the parts fit together like a puzzle. Finally you add the icing on the cake or you decorate the rooms of the house. Each of the preliminary building stages is important to the next step. Thus we will experience a building process of layer upon layer of paint as we gradually build each project.

USING OILS AND ACRYLICS

You will notice that most of the colors I use on my palette are basic standard colors in both acrylics and oils. This makes it very easy for you to paint any of these projects in the medium of your choice. You can use either acrylics or oils for any of the nine projects. My color mixes and instructions are all very similar for both mediums. Sometimes I look at the finished project and even I can't tell whether I painted that particular project in acrylics or oils.

When painting in acrylics I prefer to begin with the middle values and work toward the lighter values, then finish with the darker values. Most acrylic colors prefer to work this way, so I work with the paint. Acrylic paint is much easier to apply when being made darker. Oil paint is usually painted in the opposite order. Begin with the dark values and then add the lighter colors.

SETTING UP THE PALETTE

Since I use the same colors for both oils and acrylics, I have also found it easier for me to lay out my palette the same way for both mediums. Note how my laminated palette is laid out below. The warm colors are spaced out along the top edge of the palette from light colors to dark colors. The fewer cool colors are spaced out along the left edge of the palette. The warm and cool colors are separated with white in the upper left corner. This

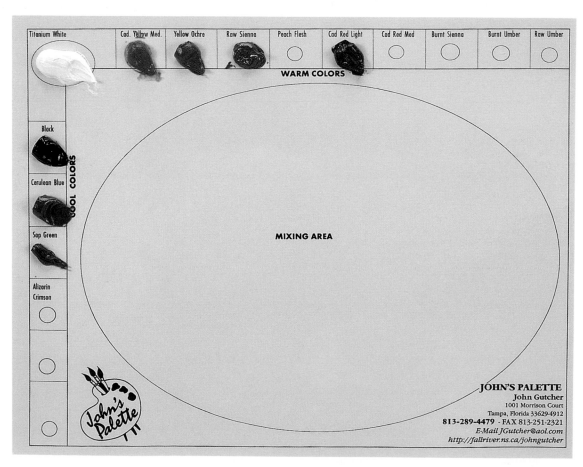

THIS IS THE PALETTE I designed for my painting and had laminated. I keep the warm colors on the top and the cool colors on the left, so I always know where they are. I mix colors in the center, and just wipe the center off when the area gets filled.

leaves the entire center area of my palette clean and open for mixing colors. When the mixing area gets filled, I can clean this area off and not have to disturb my main piles of color, which remain on the outside edges of the palette.

When I paint, I premix a series of values of each particular color right on my palette. Mix them in a straight row, either horizontally or vertically, on your palette directly below or beside the parent colors. This will help you to keep your palette organized and you will be able to easily remix more matching colors.

LOADING YOUR BRUSH

To load your flat brush, pull a small amount of paint from the bottom of the paint pile, forming a sharp chisel edge, then turn the brush over and load the other side the same way. Load a round or liner brush from the bottom of the paint pile as well, but twirl the brush between your fingers to pull the paint in a spiral toward the sharp tip of the brush.

PAINTING VALUES

Apply the paint strokes using a relatively dry brush, then mix and apply a series of lighter or darker values slightly overlapping the previous strokes. This method of applying paint will give you a gradation of color values rather than a soft, smooth blend. These value steps are like small flat planes where one color lies beside the previous patch of color. This method creates movement, excitement and vibration of the colors and values. Once the value steps are in place, the edges can be softened quite easily with the gentle sweep of a mop brush.

MAKING A GLAZE

To make some of the subtle color changes, I have used glazes. The wash or glaze can be applied over a painted area to soften edges, to darken an area or to alter the temperature of a previously painted color.

With acrylics this can be accomplished by using a blending gel and adding a small amount of color to make a transparent wash.

With oils I use RapiDry Oil Medium to make my glazes. Because this medium is very thin, it has many uses other than for making glazes. I apply a very thin layer of RapiDry to my surface before I paint. This allows my brush to glide over the surface more smoothly. I can paint wet-into-wet and all colors are automatically mixed. Most colors will tack up in about three to four hours, allowing plenty of time to blend. The colors will dry to the touch overnight, allowing me to apply additional layers the following day. The RapiDry gives my paint more gloss and brilliance, assists my brush to point up for applying finer details, acts as a glue to help the next layer of paint adhere to the previous layer, and serves as a sealer on my finished oil painting prior to varnishing. Now, does that sound wonderful? You bet it does.

a note about color mixes

To help you with mixing the values you'll need for this book, I've included a palette of color mixes at the beginning of each project. These color palettes do not include all the values you'll need to paint a given element, but they do provide touchstones for you to refer to as you're painting. Keep in mind that a realistic and lively painting comes from the layering of values. In most cases you will need to use values in between the ones on the palette to achieve a smooth and realistic look.

Three Holiday Ornaments

THESE THREE ORNAMENTS ARE BEGINNER-LEVEL PROJECTS that will introduce you to brush-mixing small amounts of color to make a series of values. Then you will be applying the paint in overlapping strokes to create gradations of colors. The projects are painted on three quite different-textured surfaces: rough slate, semi-smooth porcelain and very smooth frosted glass. All three surfaces give you a very different feel when applying the paint.

Materials

Paints

FolkArt Artists' Pigment Acrylics:
Hauser Green Dark • Hauser Green Light • Hauser Green Medium •
Napthol Crimson • Pure Black • Red Light • Titanium White • Yellow Light
FolkArt Acrylics: Mint Green • Teal Green

Brushes

Royal Fusion: 3250 no. 3 round • 3250 no. 2 round •
3585 no. 0 script liner

Additional Supplies

tracing paper • gray and white transfer paper • stylus •
J.W. etc. Right-Step Clear Matte or Gloss Varnish

Surface

Slate ornament from Bent Oak Farm • Porcelain ornament from Porcelain Treasures •
Glass ornament from Christmas By Krebs

color Mixes

Holly Leaves & Pine Needles

| Hauser Green Light | + Titanium White | Hauser Green Medium | + Titanium White | + Titanium White | Hauser Green Dark | + Titanium White |

Cardinal & Berries

| Red Light | + Yellow Light | + Yellow Light | + Yellow Light | Napthol Crimson | + Red Light |

Cardinal Eyes

| Pure Black | + Titanium White | + Titanium White |

THESE PATTERNS may be hand-traced or photocopied for personal use only. They appear here at full size.

1 Carefully trace the pattern onto a piece of tracing paper. Position the tracing paper on the surface, slide a small piece of white transfer paper under the tracing and draw the outline of the holly leaves on the slate. Base the entire image area with Titanium White. When dry, transfer the pattern for the berries with gray transfer paper.

2 Using a no. 3 round brush, base the leaves with Hauser Green Light, and base the berries with Red Light. Reposition the pattern on the surface and trace the outline of the berries and the holly veins with gray transfer paper.

3 Brush-mix a combination of Hauser Green Light and Titanium White. With a small amount of paint in the no. 3 round, paint in the veins and highlight areas of the holly leaves.

4 Begin adding darker values to the leaves with Hauser Green Medium, overlapping the areas of Hauser Green Light.

5 Darken the accent areas close to the berries with Hauser Green Dark, slightly overlapping the edges of the Hauser Green Medium to create gradations from light to dark.

6 Sharpen the light edges with more highlights using a mixture of Titanium White and Hauser Green Light.

7 Continuing with the no. 3 round, brush-mix a medium orange using Red Light and Yellow Light. Place this mixture in a circle in the upper right quadrant of each berry. Soften the edges by slightly overlapping the previous edge with more Red Light (the base coat color).

8 Add shadows to the bottoms of the berries with Napthol Crimson, softening the edges by overlapping Red Light.

9 Add a tiny Titanium White dot in the center of the highlights and soften the edge of the dot with an orange mixture.

10 Add Pure Black to accent the deep shadows around the berries. Use it to clean up any rough edges as well.

11 To finish this ornament, varnish with matte or gloss varnish.

CARDINAL
on Porcelain

1 Base the ornament with Mint Green and let dry. Position the pattern on the surface and carefully transfer it with gray transfer paper and a stylus.

With a no. 2 round, base the cardinal with Red Light, leaving blank the indications for the wing feathers. Brush-mix an orange using Red Light and Yellow Light. Base the beak and feet with this mixture.

Using Hauser Green Medium, make the center vein of the pine branches in a continuous curve. Then pull strokes out from the center vein, slightly lifting the brush from the surface to create the soft, thin outside edges of the pine needles. The strokes for the needles should be slightly curved as well.

2 Continue painting the pine needle branches, filling in the spaces between the needles close to the cardinal. As the needles project away from the cardinal they should gradually get shorter and open up a bit to create a little air between the strokes. Be sure to slightly curve each stroke as it comes out from the center vein.

3 Place a small amount of Yellow Light and Red Light on your palette, then brush-mix a series of three orange values between the two piles of paint. To create the different values, use varying amounts of each color in each mix.

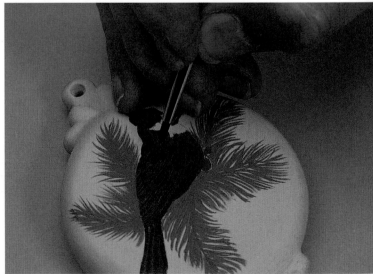

4 Begin to add the light details to the wing and tail feathers, chest and face of the cardinal. To add roundness and dimension to the feathers, begin to make tiny strokes from the outside edge, pulling in toward the center of each feather, overlapping the Red Light. Do not blend. Additional details can be painted into the beak and feet with darker orange mixtures.

5 Stroke in the shadows of the individual wing and tail feathers and around the head with Napthol Crimson, slightly overlapping the Red Light. Stroke diagonal lines in the tail feather for detail.

6 Stroke in the shadows of the pine needles with Hauser Green Dark, using the technique described in step I. Add more dark shadows directly under the cardinal.

7 Brush-mix a combination of Titanium White and Hauser Green Medium.

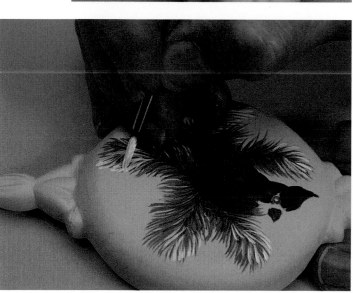

8 With this mixture, stroke in the pine needle highlights, starting from the tips and gently pulling the stroke in toward the center vein. Add these highlights at only the ends of the branches.

9 Base the eye circle with values of gray made from Pure Black and Titanium White, then place a tiny Pure Black dot in the center. Outline the eye with Pure Black and continue to fill in the face with short, choppy strokes that add texture to the face. Using Pure Black and the tip of the no. 0 script liner brush, add accent details to the beak, the underside of the body, feet and the base of the pine needles directly under the cardinal. Add Pure Black accents to the feathers, head, neck, wing and tail. Add a few accent strokes of a medium orange value and a touch of Red Light to the outside edges of the pine needles.

10 Paint the top and bottom parts of the ornament with Teal Green and varnish with matte or gloss varnish.

ORNAMENT THREE: CARDINAL
on frosted glass

This ornament is a combination of the components from the previous ornaments, and includes similar instruction for the cardinal, holly and pine needles.

1 Place a 1½-inch (3.8cm) to 2-inch (5.1cm) round template or a small paper drinking cup on the side of the round ornament and trace a circle. Position the pattern in the center of the circle and tape on two outside corners. Gently slide the transfer paper under the pattern and trace the cardinal and holly.

Base the cardinal with Red Light, the holly with Hauser Green Light and the background circle with Pure Black.

2 Mix a series of orange values made from Red Light and Yellow Light. With a light orange value, base the beak. Add details and highlights to the head, chest and wings with light and dark values of orange.

3 With a mixture of Red Light and Napthol Crimson, add shadows to the cardinal's body and tail and start to add individual feathers to the wing. Then deepen the shadows with Napthol Crimson. Base the eye, feet and twig with the Red Light and Napthol Crimson mix.

4 Add lights to the holly leaves with mixtures of Hauser Green Light and Titanium White. Add shadows to the holly leaves with Hauser Green Dark. Pull out some pine needles from behind and under the holly leaves using the same green mixtures.

5 With the no. 0 script liner brush, detail the face, eye and beak with Pure Black. Then accent some of the wing feathers, the tail, feet, twig, leaves and pine needles. Repeat a few of the accents on the leaves and pine needles with touches of orange and Red Light. This will repeat the main colors throughout the design, adding more unity. These accents could be added using a glaze made with blending gel and a small amount of color.

A glaze made with blending gel and Napthol Crimson could be used to deepen the shadows of the cardinal and add more depth to the reds.

With the script liner, add a dot of Titanium White to the eye and a highlight to the beak.

To finish this ornament, varnish with matte or gloss varnish.

Santa Portrait

THIS SANTA FACE IS AN INTRODUCTION TO PAINTING A PORTRAIT IN ACRYLICS. This study will teach you how to brush-mix flesh colors in values, then overlap those values to create gradations from light to dark. These gradations are the form, shape and roundness of the facial features. All features of a face are round—there are no sharp edges on a real face—therefore to make Santa look real, we need to paint that roundness and create the illusion of depth. We are creating a three-dimensional image on a two-dimensional surface.

Materials

Paints

FolkArt Artists' Pigment Acrylics:
Brilliant Blue • Burnt Sienna • Cerulean Blue • Ice Blue • Napthol Crimson •
Portrait • Pure Black • Raw Sienna • Red Light • Titanium White •
True Burgundy • Yellow Ochre
FolkArt Acrylics: Whipped Berry • Brilliant Blue

Brushes

Royal Fusion: 3130 no. 10 flat or 3170 filbert •
3130 no. 8 flat or 3170 filbert • 3250 no. 3 round or no. 2 round •
3585 no. 2 script liner • RG730 ⅜" (10mm) Royal Comb or ½" (12mm) Royal Comb

Additional Supplies

sandpaper • J.W. etc. First-Step Wood Sealer • tracing paper •
gray transfer paper • stylus • FolkArt Blending Gel Medium •
J.W. etc. Right-Step Clear Matte or Gloss Varnish

Surface

Wood sled from Wood Creations

color Mixes

Face & Mouth

Portrait | + Red Light + Yellow Ochre | + Titanium White | Portrait + Red Light + Raw Sienna | Red Light + Pure Black | Portrait + Titanium White

Eyes

Cerulean Blue | + Titanium White | + Titanium White

Hat

Red Light | + Yellow Medium | Red Light + Napthol Crimson | Napthol Crimson + True Burgundy

Hair & Fur

Ice Blue | + Titanium White | + Titanium White | Ice Blue + Pure Black | + Pure Black

THIS PATTERN may be hand-traced or photocopied for personal use only. Enlarge at 133 percent to bring up to full size.

PREPARATION

1 Sand the wood surface then seal with wood sealer. This will slightly raise the grain of the wood, so sand again to take the raised grain off the surface. Base the entire surface with two coats of Whipped Berry.

Position the pattern on your surface, attaching it at the two upper outside corners. Insert the transfer paper under the pattern and gently transfer the pattern using the stylus. Transfer all the pattern information to the surface for a portrait.

FLESH TONES

2 Using the no. 10 flat brush, base all the flesh areas with Portrait, leaving enough of the original drawing showing through for later painting information.

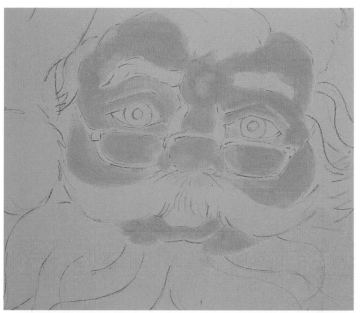

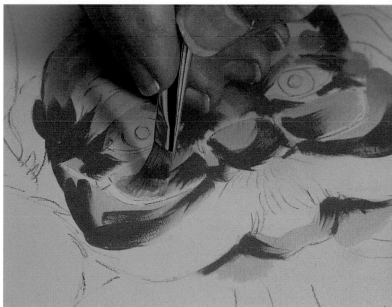

3 Brush-mix a slightly darker value by adding Red Light and Yellow Ochre to Portrait. Stroke this mixture into the shadow areas. Keep the paint slightly dry for softer dry-brush edges. Place the shadows under the eyebrows, on the sides of the nose and under the cheeks, nose and lips.

To soften the shadow areas, load the no. 8 filbert brush with a value mixture between Portrait and the shadow color. Place the brush near the edge of the shadow area, then pull the stroke into the shadow area to soften the hard edges.

4 Continue to soften the shadow edges like this, using a medium value to blend the light-valued base with the dark-valued shadow. Compare this image to that in step 3 to see what a difference the softening makes.

5 Brush-mix a slightly darker value, this time adding Raw Sienna to the Red Light and Portrait. Add these darker values under the upper eyelids; around the temples; on the sides of the lower eyelids; on the sides of the nose by the eyebrows; under the nostrils; and under the corners of the mustache.

7 Mix a glaze of Red Light and blending gel and add this glaze to the cheeks and lips for blush.

6 With the no. 2 or no. 3 round brush, fill in the opening of the mouth with Burnt Sienna. Add touches of Burnt Sienna to deepen the shadows under the mustache, at the corners of the mouth, inside the nostril holes, directly under the eyeglass rims and in the corners of the eyes.

Soften any hard edges with the previous lighter value, stroking over the edges with a dry brush. Do not try to blend smoothly or overbrush these gradations. Leave the brushstrokes showing slightly.

9 Fill in the eyeball with Titanium White on the round brush, then add a shadow under the upper eyelid with a mixture of Ice Blue and a touch of Pure Black. Soften the edge with a mixture of Ice Blue and Titanium White. (For mixing guidance, see colors for Hair & Fur on page 24.)

EYES

8 Brush-mix Titanium White and Cerulean Blue for a medium blue. Using the round brush, paint the full circles of the iris. Add a touch more Titanium White to this mixture and lighten a small area of the iris at the seven o'clock position.

10 Using straight Cerulean Blue add the shadow on the top portion of the iris under the upper eyelid. Stroke a small line of Cerulean Blue down each side of the iris and blend into the lighter blue using small strokes slanted in toward the center of the eye. These lines will appear similar to spokes on a bicycle.

11 Paint a darker shadow under the upper eyelid with Pure Black. With the no. 2 script liner, indicate the small semicircle for the tear duct muscle at the inside of the eye, then angle the line up sharply above the pupil, flatten it out slightly, then take a long gentle curve toward the outside corner, overlapping the lower eyelid. Use Pure Black to fill in the center circle for the pupil allowing equal amounts of iris to show around the pupil. Add a small black line partway down the outside edges of the iris.

EYES, CONTINUED

12 With the sharp tip of the round brush, pick up a small amount of Titanium White and place a catch light dot at the one o'clock position touching the pupil and iris. Directly across from this, at the seven o'clock position, lighten the blue iris with a mixture of Titanium White and a touch of Cerulean Blue. This will add the appearance of a wet sparkle to the eye.

EYEGLASSES

13 Base the eyeglass rims with Raw Sienna. Using the round or liner brush, add a light line to the top edges of the rims with Yellow Ochre. Add a thin shadow line on the bottom rim edges with Burnt Sienna. Add a few Pure Black accents at the outside corners of the rims and at the points where the rims touch the nostrils. Add Titanium White sparkle highlights to the top surfaces of the rims.

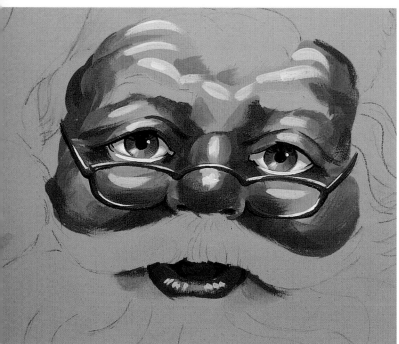

FINAL FACE DETAILS

14 With a lighter mixture of Portrait and Titanium White, add a few highlights to the top edges of the face wrinkles, on the cheeks and lips and on the tip of the nose. Add a few more shadows inside and under the mouth with a mixture of Red Light and a touch of Pure Black (or you could use straight Burnt Umber). The face is now complete.

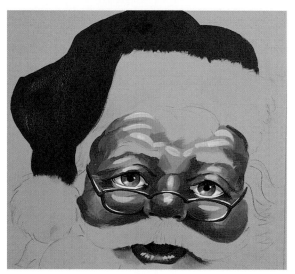

BRIGHT RED HAT

15 Red is a very difficult color to paint with acrylics and keep it looking bright. Try this formula: First base the entire hat with Red Light on the no. 10 filbert.

> *Tip*
>
> *T*he hat is made of wool, a rough-textured material. Try to capture the texture of wool by leaving the brush strokes showing when you overlap the edges. Do not use a mop brush to blend the strokes.

16 Make a mixture of Red Light and Cadmium Yellow Medium for a rich red-orange. With this mixture, highlight the top front areas of the hat wrinkles using a flat or filbert brush and stroking the color across the highlights. Soften the edges by overlapping them with more Red Light. Leave the texture and brushstrokes showing. Stroke some Napthol Crimson into the shadow areas; overlap the edges with more Red Light.

17 Deepen the shadows with True Burgundy, overlapping the edges with Napthol Crimson. This simple gradation of reds will give you four definite values with gradations in between to give the illusion of roundness.

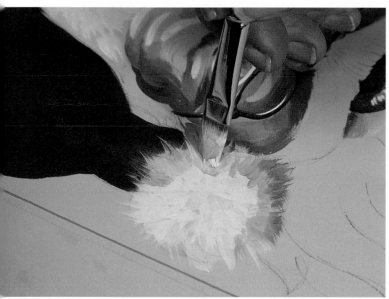

SOFT FUR

18 The layering of values and the use of fan-shaped strokes are the keys to the soft fur on the hat's tassel and rim. As shown in the diagram at right, the strokes are layered, slightly darker ones at the bottom, lighter ones at the top. Use the flat side of the filbert brush to begin to stroke Ice Blue around the outside edge of the tassel. Pull the stroke outward in a small fan shape, lifting the brush away from the surface to create a dry-brush edge. Make more strokes, placing them close enough to slightly overlap each other. Add a bit of Titanium White to the Ice Blue for a medium value, and paint strokes overlapping the dark value.

BRUSHSTROKES FOR FUR

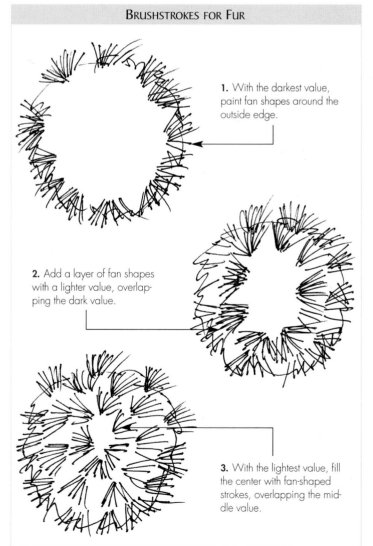

1. With the darkest value, paint fan shapes around the outside edge.

2. Add a layer of fan shapes with a lighter value, overlapping the dark value.

3. With the lightest value, fill the center with fan-shaped strokes, overlapping the middle value.

FUR, CONTINUED

19 Finish the bottom layer of Ice Blue, then finish the medium layer of Ice Blue and Titanium White. Add more Titanium White to the medium-value mix, and add more overlapping rows.

20 Using the same stroke, brush in the center with layers of Titanium White for the highlight, overlapping the previous layers.

RIM OF HAT & EYEBROWS

21 The rim of the hat is done similarly to the tassel. Begin with a row of the darkest value, this time Ice Blue plus a touch of Pure Black, and continue overlapping with progressively lighter values as you paint in toward the center. Finish with Titanium White in the center area. Use a very light touch to carry some of the white into the background and onto the red of the hat.

For the eyebrows, use the flat edge of the filbert brush and stroke in some shadows under the eyebrows with Ice Blue and a touch of Pure Black. Add more Titanium White and paint lighter values as you work toward the top of the eyebrows. Stroke in the few highlights on the top edge of the eyebrows with Titanium White. Some of these highlights can be painted with the script liner.

HAIR

22 With a mixture of Ice Blue and a touch of Pure Black on the no. 8 filbert brush, stroke in the flowing waves of the hair shadows on the sides of the head and in the center of the forehead. Refer to the illustration on page 31 for more information on painting hair.

23 With Ice Blue and a touch of Titanium White, add some lighter values to the upper portions of the hair. Use the edge of a very dry brush to help create the look of hair.

24 Add bright Titanium White highlights to the top edges of the hair. To add a bit of detail, use thinned Titanium White in the script liner brush and create a few individual hairs. This will give you sharp line details. Less is better, so don't overdo the highlights.

MUSTACHE

25 Start with the dark mixture of Ice Blue and Pure Black and paint the dark values under the mustache. Continue to use the dry no. 8 filbert to create the hair.

BRUSHSTROKES FOR HAIR

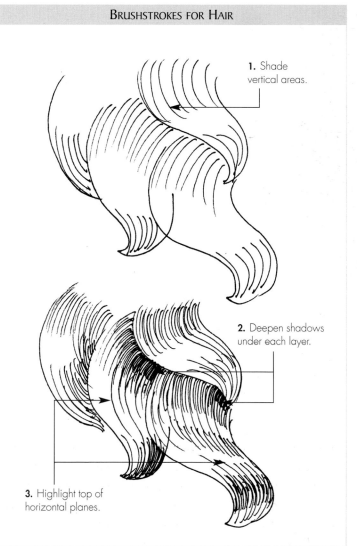

1. Shade vertical areas.

2. Deepen shadows under each layer.

3. Highlight top of horizontal planes.

MUSTACHE, CONTINUED

26 Brush some Ice Blue shadows into the lower portion of the mustache from under the nose, stroking out toward the left and out toward the right. Continue adding more Titanium White for lighter values toward the top of the mustache.

27 Add lighter values with more Titanium White, then add details on the upper portion of the mustache with the script liner. Pull just a couple of stray curved hairs down over the shadow of the mouth for realism.

LONG FLOWING BEARD

28 Using the no. 10 flat brush and Ice Blue, begin to form the long flowing strokes for the wavy beard. Paint long S strokes, starting with the chisel edge of the brush, pushing down with more pressure for a wider stroke, then lifting up and away from the surface. Refer to the pattern for the shapes and position of the overlapping layers of the beard.

29 Fill in the larger shapes with Ice Blue, leaving the outline of the shapes as the background color. Notice the strokes are shorter and layered under the mouth and in the center and larger toward the outside edges. Most of the strokes will curve to the left on the left side and curve right on the right side. The strokes at the bottom of the beard merge in toward the center.

30 Using a ½-inch (12mm) or ⅜-inch (10mm) comb brush, add more details and more hair to the beard with a mixture of Titanium White and Ice Blue. Let some of the previous layers show through.

31 Begin adding more light values to the center portion of the beard directly under the mouth. Gradually build thicker layers of Titanium White in the center area, adding more Titanium White after the previous layer has dried so that the whitest highlights are very bright. Leave the outer and lower edges of the beard slightly darker. This will create the illusion of roundness and depth in the overall beard.

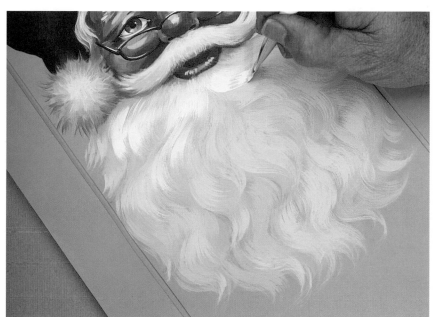

32 When the beard is dry, add more details using a script liner and thinned Titanium White. Add a few single hairs in the front of the beard and on the eyebrows and mustache. The Santa portrait is now complete. He is alive, he has form and he has roundness.

33 Finish the project by painting the edges of the pieces of the sled with Brilliant Blue. Varnish with matte or gloss varnish.

Angel

THIS GLORIOUS ANGEL MAKES A WONDERFUL KEEPSAKE BOX to bring joy to your world. Pastel colors, soft flowing feathers and sweeping folds abound as she announces her coming amidst boughs of holly and berries.

Materials

Paints

FolkArt Artists' Pigment Acrylics:
Burnt Sienna • Burnt Umber • Hauser Green Medium • Ice Blue • Napthol Crimson • Portrait • Pure Black • Raw Sienna • Red Light • Titanium White • Yellow Ochre

FolkArt Acrylics: Pure Gold Metallic

Brushes

Royal Fusion: 3130 no. 10 flat or 3170 filbert • 3130 no. 8 flat or 3170 filbert • 3130 no. 6 flat or 3170 filbert • 3250 no. 3 round • 3585 no. 2 script liner

Additional Supplies

tracing paper • gray transfer paper • stylus • sea sponge • J.W. etc. Right-Step Clear Matte or Gloss Varnish

Surface

Bisque round box from Porcelain Treasures

color Mixes

Wings

Ice Blue + Titanium White + Burnt Umber | + Burnt Umber | Ice Blue + Titanium White | + Titanium White

Flesh

Portrait | + Titanium White | + Titanium White | Portrait + Red Light | + Burnt Sienna | + Burnt Sienna

Dress

Red Light + Titanium White + Burnt Sienna | + Titanium White | Red Light + Burnt Sienna | + Titanium White | + Titanium White

Hair

Yellow Ochre | + Titanium White | Yellow Ochre + Burnt Umber

Horn

Yellow Ochre + Raw Sienna | + Titanium White | Yellow Ochre + Burnt Sienna

THIS PATTERN may be hand-traced or photocopied for personal use only. The pattern appears here at full size.

Preparation & Background

1 Usually bisque or porcelain does not need to be prepped. The surface will have a slight tooth allowing the paint to grab onto and bind to the surface.

Position the pattern on the surface, then with a soft, gray transfer paper under the pattern, trace the pattern with a stylus, transferring it to the surface.

Base the berries with Red Light and the holly leaves with Hauser Green Medium using the no. 3 round. Base the background with Pure Black. Follow the instructions in project 1 (page 15) to complete the holly berries and leaves.

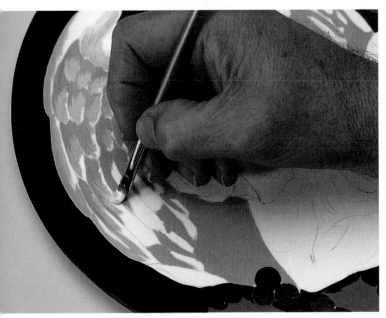

3 Lighten the shadow mixture with more Titanium White and Ice Blue. Still using the chisel edge of the no. 6 brush, begin to stroke in the light/middle value of the feathers. Stroke in toward the center of each feather, leaving some of the porcelain showing for highlights.

Wings

2 Using the chisel edge of the no. 6 flat or filbert brush, begin to fill in the shadows under each of the wing feathers with a mixture of Titanium White, Ice Blue and a touch of Burnt Umber. This will give you a light, warm gray.

4 Finish adding the light/middle value to both wings. Notice that each row of feathers is layered from the top down. The lower tips of the feathers are light, then they gradually get darker as they go under the previous layer, which is darker still.

5 Now start adding more darks and details to the undersides of the feathers. Darken the base color slightly with more Burnt Umber. Draw a center vein in each feather, and then pull in small strokes from each side toward the center using the chisel edge of the no. 6 brush. Paint one feather at a time starting with the feathers in the upper shadows. This will begin to make the layers more prominent.

6 The undersides of the feather layers are now darker and the feather details are in place. Soften the outside edges of the upper shoulder portion of the wings with a mixture of Ice Blue and Titanium White. These upper shoulders are lightest because they project forward and are at the tops of the wings.

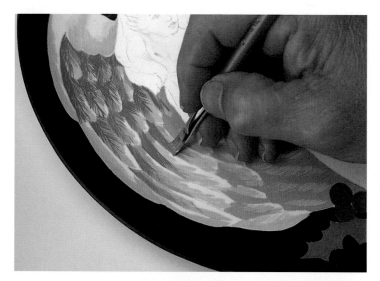

7 Using the round brush, sharpen the highlight details at the ends of each feather with more Titanium White added to the previous mix. Also lighten the highlight on the tops of the wing shoulders with more white.

8 You now have a full range of values in the wings. The upper shoulders are bright and lighter in value; the shadows under the shoulder and under each of the feathers are darker values.

FOLDS IN THE DRESS

9 Brush-mix a medium/light shadow color with Titanium White, Red Light and a touch of Burnt Sienna. Don't mix this color too dark in the beginning because acrylic paint dries a value darker and prefers to be made darker rather than lighter—you can make it darker later if you need to. Base only the shadows of the dress, according to the photo, with either the no. 8 or the no. 10 flat or filbert brush. Immediately you are aware of value and of the large mass areas of shadows and of lights.

11 Add slightly more Red Light and Burnt Sienna to your original mixture for a slightly darker value and darken some of the deeper shadows. Again overlap the edges of two values with an in-between value for a soft gradation.

10 Add more Titanium White to your mixture and base in the light areas of the dress. Leave some of the porcelain showing through as highlight areas. Where the light value touches the darker value, brush-mix an in-between value and overlap the edges to create a soft gradation of values. Brush in the direction of the folds with the flat side of the brush.

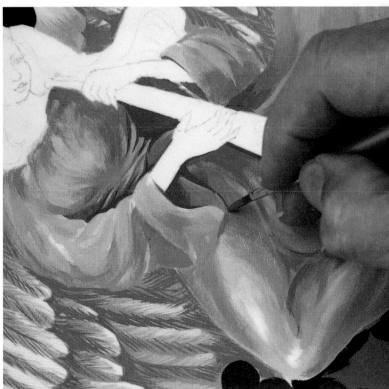

12 Using the round brush, begin to draw in the details to define the edges of the angel's sleeves, waist, chest and sharp folds in the dress.

FOLDS IN THE DRESS, CONTINUED

13 With the no. 8 or no. 10 brush, add more highlights to the frontal planes and folds of the dress using a highlight mixture of Titanium White and the lightest value mix (used in step 10). Soften all edges using a flat dry brush and combing over the edges with either a lighter or darker value.

14 Paint the decorative design at the bottom of the dress with the round brush and a mixture of Red Light and a touch of Burnt Sienna. Tap in a continuous line following the shape of the dress edges.

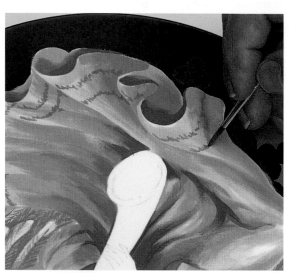

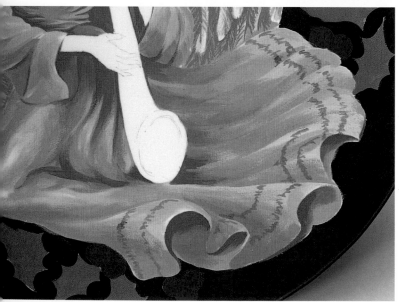

15 The detail lines naturally will be lighter (by adding more Titanium White to the base color) on the top highlight planes of the dress and darker (by adding more Burnt Sienna to the base color) as the design goes into shadow. Even the dotted design follows the same relative value changes as the lights and darks of the dress folds.

FACE, HAIR & HORN

16 Base the flesh, face and hands with Portrait. Leave some of the drawing detail showing through for later reference. Base the hair with Yellow Ochre. Base the horn with a mixture of Yellow Ochre and a touch of Raw Sienna.

17 Add Titanium White to Portrait and paint in the highlights on the face and hands.

Add Titanium White to the Yellow Ochre and highlight the hair. Add Titanium White to the horn mixture and paint the highlights in the center and on the top rim of the horn.

Make the initial crosses for the stars with Ice Blue using the round brush or a no. 2 liner brush. The cross will have a longer center vertical stroke and a shorter horizontal stroke.

18 Now that the highlights have been added to the middle values of the flesh, add the darker values and the details. Darken the Portrait with touches of Burnt Sienna and Red Light. Brush-mix this darker value using the round brush, then add the eyebrows, details of the eyes, and shadows under the nose and chin. Paint the top lip with Burnt Sienna and the lower lip with Red Light, highlighted with Titanium White. Add the same darker values to the hands, then add a touch more Burnt Sienna for the dividing sections of the fingers.

Add Burnt Umber to the Yellow Ochre for the hair and stroke in the shadow details. Use straight Burnt Umber for the shadow around the face and under the waves of hair.

Add Burnt Sienna to the shadows of the horn, overlapping each value for a slightly blended gradation of values.

For the stars, add the diagonal cross lines with Ice Blue, then add random-sized dots around the stars.

19 Basecoat the sides of the box with Pure Black. Dip the sea sponge into Pure Gold Metallic. Tap the sponge on the palette to distribute the paint, then tap the sponge lightly around the edge of the lid, on the sides of the lid and on the sides of the box.

To complete this project, varnish with matte or gloss varnish.

Santa's List

THIS CHARACTER TAKES ON THE FEEL OF AN OLD RENAISSANCE SANTA as he leans over his desk, checking off with his quill pen the names on his delivery list. Painting this project will help you to centralize the focus area to Santa's face and to the soft texture of the quill pen. The background is dark with a glazed antique border. The outside edges of the box are sponged with Burnt Umber over a base of metallic gold for an old-world antique appearance.

Materials

Paints

FolkArt Artists' Pigment Acrylics:
Burnt Sienna • Burnt Umber • Hauser Green Medium • Ice Blue •
Napthol Crimson • Portrait • Pure Black • Raw Sienna • Red Light •
Titanium White • True Burgundy • Yellow Ochre
FolkArt Acrylics: Pure Gold Metallic

Brushes

Royal Fusion: 3130 no. 6 flat or 3170 filbert •
3250 no. 3 round • 3585 no. 2 script liner

Additional Supplies

sandpaper • J.W. etc. First-Step Wood Sealer • tracing paper •
gray transfer paper • stylus • FolkArt Blending Gel Medium • sea sponge •
J.W. etc. Right-Step Clear Matte or Gloss Varnish

Surface

Curved Top Jewelry Box by Wayne's Woodenware, Inc.

Color Mixes

Face & Hands

Portrait | + Red Light + Yellow Ochre | + Titanium White | Portrait + Burnt Sienna | + Burnt Umber | Portrait + Titanium White

Shirt

Hauser Green Medium + Titanium White | + Titanium White | Hauser Green Medium + Pure Black | Hauser Green Medium + Burnt Umber + Titanium White

Hair & Beard

Ice Blue + Titanium White | + Titanium White | Ice Blue + Pure Black | + Pure Black

Signboard & Tabletop

   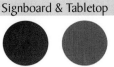

Ice Blue + Burnt Umber | + Burnt Umber | Burnt Sienna to Yellow Ochre | Raw Sienna + Yellow Ochre + Titanium White | Yellow Ochre to Titanium White | Burnt Umber + Titanium White

THIS PATTERN may be hand-traced or photocopied for personal use only. Enlarge at 125 percent to bring it up to full size.

PREPARATION

1 Sand the surface, then seal with wood sealer. Let dry and sand again. Transfer the pattern onto the surface using gray transfer paper and a stylus.

Base the sides of the surface and the entire background around the figure and table with Burnt Umber. Base the wood frame, table and hourglass design areas with Raw Sienna.

3 Brush-mix darker flesh values by adding Burnt Sienna to the above mixture. Using the no. 3 round brush add the shadow details of the face, under the nose, around the mouth and between the fingers. Overlap these dark values to soften the edges.

Tip

*B*efore you completely finish the flesh tones, it is a good idea to at least base in as much surrounding color as possible. The colors of the background and clothing will have an effect on both the values and intensity of the flesh colors.

FACE & HANDS

2 Base the face and hands with Portrait. Leave open some of the pattern drawing for the main features of the face and hands. Brush-mix a small amount of a darker value using Red Light and Yellow Ochre added to the Portrait. Paint this mixture into the shadow areas of the face and hands. Overlap the edges with a mixture in-between to soften the edges.

4 Continuing to add values for shape and form, mix a touch more Red Light to the basic flesh mixture of Red Light, Yellow Ochre and Portrait. Use this mixture to add more color to the lips, more detail around the eyes and to the wrinkles on the sides of the forehead.

Add a touch of Burnt Umber to the mixture in step 3 for more accent shadows. Soften all edges of the warm flesh colors, especially those around the nose and on the cheeks, with a small amount of Red Light. Add a light mixture of Titanium White and Portrait for the highlights.

HAT & VEST

5 Base the hat and vest with Red Light. Fill in the shadow areas with Napthol Crimson and blend the edges with additional layers of Red Light.

6 Deepen the hat and vest shadows with True Burgundy, then soften the edges with Napthol Crimson in the middle values.

SHIRT

7 Brush-mix Hauser Green Medium and Titanium White for the shadows of the shirt. Fill in the light areas with a mixture of the above plus more Titanium White. Both of these are quite light values of soft green. Be sure to add some of this shirt color inside the hourglass.

8 Mix darker values by adding more Hauser Green Medium to the first mix. Brush these mixes in the shadows, slightly overlapping the lighter values for soft edges. The shadows will be darkest directly under the arms, in the creases of the sleeves and under the curves of the vest.

9 Now add the darkest cast shadows. Mix Hauser Green Medium plus a tiny amount of Pure Black. With the round brush, add spots of cast shadow on the sleeve, inside the cuffs, under the tassel and in the corner of the hourglass.

10 Brush-mix Titanium White and Ice Blue and begin to shape the long waves of the beard, mustache and hair. Tap this color into the shadows of the pompom. Add more Titanium White to the mix and stroke in the highlights. Use short fan-shaped strokes for the pompom and long, flowing strokes for the beard (refer to project two for more information about these strokes).

11 Add a touch of Pure Black to the Ice Blue for the shadow values and stroke in the shadows on the underside of the beard, hair and mustache. Tap this darker shadow onto the lower edges of the pompom.

Add Titanium White to the mix for highlights in the areas close to the face, then add more Titanium White to the center areas for the brightest highlights.

EYEGLASSES

12 Add a few individual hairs to the beard with Titanium White on the script liner.

Base the eyeglasses with Yellow Ochre. Using the script liner, add Titanium White highlights to the top edges of the glasses. Use Burnt Umber for the shadows under each of the rims.

FINAL TOUCHES ON FACE & HANDS

13 At this point the areas around the face are complete, so any additional details and color shifts to the flesh tones can be made. Rather than repaint areas to darken them, mix a glaze of blending gel and a small amount of Burnt Sienna. Wash this glaze over the deep shadows, the creases of the face and between the fingers to give them more depth.

With a touch of Titanium White, add the brightest highlights to the eyelids, nose, forehead and eyebrows.

SIGNBOARD & FEATHER

14 Base the notepaper and calendar with Titanium White; this base coat will show through for the highlights. Paint the shadows of the notepaper, calendar and the feather with a mixture of Ice Blue and Titanium White.

15 Add a touch of Pure Black to the Ice Blue for some darker shading on the notepaper and on the calendar behind the feather. Add Burnt Umber to the Ice Blue for a warmer shading color for the individual detail lines of the feather. Make these strokes long, flowing curves toward the center vein of the feather.

16 Highlight the center vein of the feather with Titanium White, then gently backstroke some Titanium White details from the center vein outward, overlapping the darker values. This will soften the edges of the feather even more.

The pen nib is metal, so it has very high contrast and is painted with sharp-edged values. Paint the cast shadows under the tip with Pure Black, add bright highlights in vertical strokes with Titanium White, then add a few middle-value gray shadows on the backside of the pen nib.

17 To add dimension to the notepaper, use straight Titanium White to paint a turned-up corner or ripple. Finish the calendar by lettering the type and the large "24" with Napthol Crimson. Draw in the hash marks with a mixture of Ice Blue and Burnt Umber.

Base the corner pushpins with Ice Blue, then add the shadow details with Pure Black and the highlights with Titanium White.

Add wood grain to the signboard with Burnt Sienna, Burnt Umber and a mixture of the two for the deeper cast shadows under the white pages.

18 To bring the book and papers forward in the painting, the colors of these elements will be warmer than those on the calendar. Base the papers and the book with Ice Blue and a touch of Burnt Umber. Shade the side of the book and under the pages with a mixture of Ice Blue and more Burnt Umber. Base the inkwell with a mixture of Titanium White and Pure Black. This will be enough of a cooler gray color to keep the inkwell in the background.

19 Add more Pure Black to the mix and shade the curved top on the inkwell bottle, then add lighter values on the outside edges. Detail the inkwell with straight Pure Black. With Burnt Umber add more shadow details to the book cover and pages.

20 Add grain to the tabletop with Burnt Sienna, using dry brushstrokes and the chisel edge of the filbert brush.

TABLE, CONTINUED

21 Darken the cast shadows under the book and on the very front edge of the tabletop with Burnt Umber. Lighten the front top edge of the tabletop with a mixture of Burnt Sienna and Yellow Ochre. This is called "dramatizing the values" to create more of an illusion of depth. On a sharp edge where the light meets the dark, the light top edge will be lighter, and the dark front edge will be darker. For another example of this, see the gift boxes in project seven.

HOURGLASS

22 The wood frame of the hourglass has already been based with Raw Sienna. Now add dark wood grain with Burnt Sienna using wavy strokes. Add lighter grain strokes with graduating values of Raw Sienna and Yellow Ochre plus a touch of Titanium White.

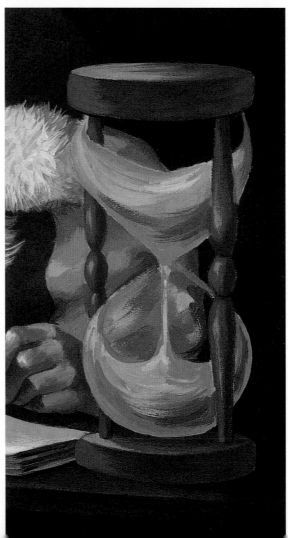

24 Add more shadows to the sand with values made darker by adding more Burnt Umber to the mix. Soften the gradations of the sand with middle values, then add the lights with values made by adding more Titanium White to the original mix.

23 Add additional highlights to the front edges of the wood with a mixture of Yellow Ochre and Titanium White.

Add shadows to the sand with a series of values of Titanium White and Burnt Umber. Tap this color in with the tip of the round brush to create texture.

25 Using a very dry brush and paint, begin to add some high-contrast strokes to the glass portion of the hourglass. Add a few hints of green reflections on the glass with a mix of Hauser Green Medium plus Burnt Umber and Titanium White. Mix a glaze of blending gel and Burnt Sienna and add a few warmer strokes. Finally add Titanium White strokes for some sharp bright highlights to make the glass shine. Paint these on the front outside edge, then follow the curve of the glass shape for the inside edges.

26 Dip the sea sponge into Pure Gold Metallic, then tap the sponge on your palette to distribute the paint. Tap the sponge on the sides of the lid and box, turning the sponge to vary the pattern. (The sides of the box are shown in the image on page 43.)

To complete this project, varnish with either matte or gloss varnish.

St. Nick

Iɴ ᴛʜɪѕ ᴅᴇѕɪɢɴ, ᴀɴ ᴏʟᴅ ᴡᴏʀʟᴅ Sᴛ. Nɪᴄᴋ ᴍᴀᴋᴇѕ ʜɪѕ ᴡᴀʏ ᴛʜʀᴏᴜɢʜ ᴛʜᴇ ᴄᴏʟᴅ, dark night checking his location with the use of his lantern. The warm glow of the lantern is concentrated on the signpost and St. Nick's face. A high contrast of colors and values adds to the drama of the scene. The bright reds of the long flowing robe are a great lesson on painting convincing deep-red objects.

Materials

Paints

FolkArt Artists' Pigment Acrylics: Burnt Sienna • Burnt Umber • Cobalt • Hauser Green Dark • Hauser Green Medium • Ice Blue • Napthol Crimson • Portrait • Pure Black • Raw Sienna • Red Light • Titanium White • True Burgundy • Yellow Light • Yellow Ochre

FolkArt Acrylics: Pure Gold Metallic • Blue Bonnet • Hunter Green

Brushes

Royal Fusion: 3130 no. 6 flat or 3170 filbert • 3250 no. 3 round • 3585 no. 2 script liner

Additional Supplies

sandpaper • J.W. etc. First-Step Wood Sealer • ruler • pencil • blue low-tack masking tape • razor blade or X-Acto Knife • tracing paper • gray transfer paper • stylus • sea sponge • FolkArt Blending Gel Medium • J.W. etc. Right-Step Clear Matte or Gloss Varnish

Surface

Wood signboard from Woodcraft

color Mixes

Signpost

 Raw Sienna
 + Titanium White
 + Titanium White
 Burnt Umber
 + Raw Sienna

Snow

 Ice Blue
 + Cobalt
 + Cobalt
 + Pure Black
+ Pure Black

Scroll

Burnt Sienna
 + Titanium White
+ Titanium White

Mittens

 Hauser Green Medium
 + Titanium White
 Hauser Green Medium + Pure Black

Robe

 Red Light
 + Yellow Light
 + Yellow Light
 Napthol Crimson + Red Light
 True Burgundy

Flesh

 Portrait
 Red Light + Yellow Ochre + Titanium White
 + Red Light
 + Red Light
 + Burnt Sienna

THIS PATTERN may be hand-traced or photocopied for personal use only. Enlarge at 200 percent to bring it up to full size.

BASECOAT & PREPARATION

1 Sand the surface, then seal it with wood sealer. Let dry, then sand again.

Using a ruler and sharp pencil, measure in from the edges 1½ inches (3.8cm) and 1¾ inches (4.5cm), which will make a ¼-inch (0.6cm) inside border. Connect the lines and tape around this inside border with blue low-tack masking tape. Paint this inside border with three coats of Pure Gold Metallic acrylic. When the border is completely dry, carefully take off the masking tape.

Transfer the pattern onto the surface with transfer paper and a stylus. There will be a few areas of the design that will overlap the gold border and project into the outside margin area. Basecoat the outside margin area with Hunter Green, outlining around the design areas that project into the margin. Basecoat the upper and lower signboard panels with Blue Bonnet.

2 Tap a small sea sponge into a puddle of Pure Gold Metallic acrylic, tap the sponge on your palette to smooth out the distribution of paint on the sponge, then gently tap on the inside area of the signboard top and bottom panels. Twist and turn the sponge so the pattern does not repeat itself. Soften the edges as it overlaps the blue base coat. Let some of the blue show through; do not fill in solid with the gold.

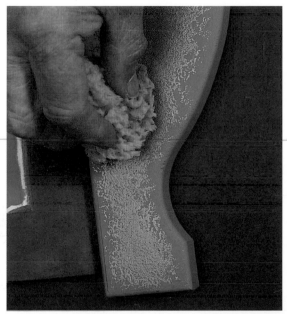

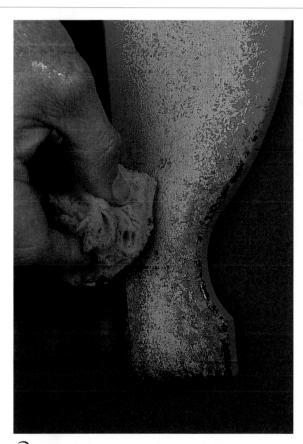

3 Using another section of the dry sponge, tap into both Blue Bonnet and a small amount of Pure Black. This will give you a mottled color on the sponge. Gently tap the edges of the sponged gold center section to soften the edge. Again, leave some of the original blue base coat showing through.

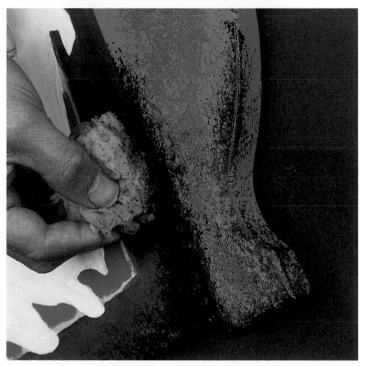

4 Now with only Pure Black on the sponge, tap the inside edges and corners of the board. This will overlap the blue/black sponged edge and will also overlap the green margin almost up to the gold inside border.

Signpost

5 Base the signpost with light values of Raw Sienna and Titanium White. Add more Titanium White to the mix for the lightest value areas near the top of the post, on the larger sign and under the sign arms. Base the lantern light and the snow areas of the post and the trees with Titanium White.

6 Base the shadow side of the post with Raw Sienna. Continue adding slightly darker mixtures of Raw Sienna and Titanium White for more shadows under the snow on the cross posts and on the front edges. Shade the left side of the sign and the bottom right side of the post with slightly darker Raw Sienna and Titanium White mixes. Stroke the values in these areas creating the wood texture by overlapping the strokes of light and dark values.

Base the trees under the snow areas with Hauser Green Medium.

7 Base the background sky behind the post and trees with Blue Bonnet.

Using a no. 3 round brush, begin to add more wood grain in the shadow areas of the signpost with Burnt Sienna strokes, then add darker shadow values with Burnt Umber.

Add Pure Black accent shadows directly under the snow, under the branches of the trees and in the foreground under the robe.

8 Add more darks and details to the wood grain in the shadows with Raw Sienna and Burnt Umber; add more wood details to the highlight areas with a mixture of Titanium White and Raw Sienna. Lighten the front edge of the post next to the dark shadow.

9 With Pure Black add the darkest accents to the wood grain at the front shadow edge where it touches the light. For more contrast and depth, add Pure Black accents in the small corners under the snow.

10 Using the no. 3 round brush and Raw Sienna, add the lettering to the signposts. I named my street corners "Joy" and "Peace." You could add your street name or your own name to the signboard. If the lettering blends in with the background color, lighten it slightly with a touch of Titanium White.

11 Using the no. 2 script liner add highlights of Titanium White to the top and left sides of the lettering. Add the shadows to the bottom and right sides of the lettering with Burnt Umber.

SNOW

12 Begin tapping Ice Blue shadows onto the snow on the upper back edges of the signboard and on the lower left edges of the trees. Mix a slightly darker value of Ice Blue plus Cobalt, then mix an even darker value by adding a touch of Pure Black, to reduce the intensity of the color, and add shadows to the outer edges of the snow. The trees gradually get darker as they recede into the distance, so add more shadows to these trees. Cover up more of the snow on the near distant trees behind the signpost, but leave a small amount of white showing through. Add more shadows to the most distant trees, so no white shows.

13 Add a touch more Pure Black to the shadow mix and tap in more shadows.

14 Mix a very light, warm glaze using blending gel and a tiny amount of Burnt Sienna. Place this glaze over some of the white highlights and some of the shadows. This will add a warm glow that would be coming from the lantern.

15 Load the tip of your no. 3 round brush with Titanium White. Tap in some sparkle dots primarily in the light areas, then scatter a few over the shadows of the foreground trees.

SANTA & SCROLL

16 Base the inside of the scroll with a medium mix of Burnt Sienna and Titanium White. Add more Titanium White to the mix for the top highlights of the scroll. Add more Burnt Sienna for a slightly darker value to begin the shadows under the rolls of the scroll.

Base all of Santa's hair, fur and beard with Titanium White.

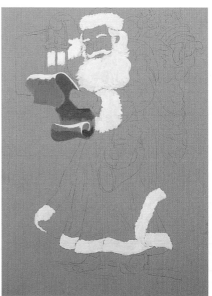

17 Base the hat and robe with Red Light. Use long strokes to paint the robe, and leave open the lines that show the robe divisions.

18 Make a light mix of Hauser Green Medium and Titanium White, then basecoat the mittens, shoes, small tree and joker's shirt. With Portrait, base St. Nick's face, the dolls' faces and the cracker. Begin painting some of the toys with Yellow Ochre and Raw Sienna.

19 Fill in the remainder of the background sky with Blue Bonnet. Base the horn and lantern with Yellow Ochre. Base the bag with Burnt Sienna in the shadows and Raw Sienna in the highlights. Base the belt with Cobalt. Darken the shadows on the ground with a mix of Hauser Green Dark and a touch of Pure Black. Add shadows to the mittens with a mix of Hauser Green Medium and a touch of Pure Black.

Add Titanium White and a touch of Yellow Ochre to Portrait and add the highlights on the front of the face, forehead, nose and cheeks.

ROBE

20 Mix a bright red-orange using Red Light and Yellow Light. Apply long, flowing highlights to the robe, softening the edges with more Red Light.

21 Brush-mix Napthol Crimson and Red Light and add the middle shadow values to the robe and hat.

22 Gradually add darker values to the shadows, overlapping each value for a gradation of color. Brush-mix Napthol Crimson and True Burgundy for the deepest shadows.

23 Add a touch of Pure Black to the True Burgundy and darken the cast shadows directly under the scroll, sleeves and horn. Deepen the shadows on the back right side and under the waist as well.

FACE & BEARD

24 Next, create more shape and roundness to the face by adding more middle and shadow values. Brush-mix Red Light, Yellow Ochre and a touch of Titanium White for the middle values around the forehead, cheeks, nose and ear. Add a touch of Burnt Sienna to this mix for deeper shadows and creases in the face. Add a touch more Red Light for blush in the cheeks.

25 Add Titanium White highlights to the tip of the nose and the upper edges of the forehead creases. Base the iris and pupil with Raw Sienna. Fill in the eyeballs with Ice Blue. Place a spot of Pure Black in the center of the iris for the pupil. Thin the Pure Black with blending gel and glaze in shadows under the upper eyelids, under the eyebrows, under the nose, in the nostrils and on outside corners of the mouth directly under the mustache.

26 Using a no. 3 round brush and Ice Blue, begin to add the shadows to the hair, beard and fur. Use long strokes for the hair, mustache, eyebrows and beard; use short tapping strokes for the fur on the cap and cuffs. Add Titanium White to the Ice Blue for lighter values, and then add straight Titanium White for the highlights. Soften and overlap each value as you paint from the shadows up to the bright highlights.

27 Add a touch of Pure Black to the Ice Blue for the shadows. Add more Pure Black for the deepest accent shadows on the right shadow side of the face and beard and around the hand holding the scroll.

FINISHING TOUCHES

$\mathscr{28}$ For the golden glow of the lantern, highlight the center with Titanium White, then gradually add darker values with Yellow Light, then Yellow Ochre. Base the top of the lantern with Yellow Ochre, add shadows with Raw Sienna, and add accent details with Burnt Sienna. Paint the toys with soft muted color mixes, as described below, to keep them in the background.

Follow the instructions in project one for painting the holly leaves and berries. To finish this project, varnish with matte or gloss varnish.

① **Ball and joker's hat:** straight color and mixtures of Yellow Ochre and Red Light.

② **Doll hair and inside the drum:** straight color and mixtures of Yellow Ochre and Raw Sienna.

③ **Doll dress:** straight color and mixtures of Cobalt, Pure Black and Titanium White.

④ **Tree, joker's jacket and cracker bands and ends:** straight color and mixtures of Hauser Green Medium, Pure Black and Yellow Ochre.

⑤ **Drum band:** straight color and mixtures of Burnt Sienna, Pure Black and Raw Sienna.

⑥ **Horn:** straight color and mixtures of Raw Sienna, Burnt Sienna, Yellow Ochre and Titanium White; outline with Burnt Umber.

⑦ **Cracker:** straight Portrait and mixtures of Titanium White and Ice Blue.

Santa & Mrs. Claus

Tʜᴇ ꜰᴏᴄᴜꜱ ᴏꜰ ᴛʜɪꜱ ᴄᴏᴍꜰʏ ꜱᴄᴇɴᴇ ɪꜱ Sᴀɴᴛᴀ ᴀɴᴅ Mʀꜱ. Cʟᴀᴜꜱ relaxing in the warm glow coming from their fireplace. All the joys of Christmas are around them—the Christmas tree, the decorated mantle in the background with their stockings hung over the fireplace, the long-awaited gift boxes and the teddy bear leaning on the armchair.

Materials

Paints

FolkArt Artists' Pigment Acrylics:

Alizarin Crimson • Burnt Sienna • Burnt Umber • Cerulean Blue • Cobalt •
Hauser Green Medium • Hauser Green Dark • Ice Blue • Napthol Crimson • Portrait •
Pure Black • Pure Orange • Raw Sienna • Red Light • Titanium White •
Yellow Light • Yellow Ochre

Brushes

Royal Fusion: 3130 no. 6 flat or 3170 filbert •
3250 no. 3 round • 3585 no. 2 script liner

Additional Supplies

sandpaper • J.W. etc. First-Step Wood Sealer • ruler • pencil •
blue low-tack masking tape • sea sponge • tracing paper • gray transfer paper •
stylus • FolkArt Blending Gel Medium • J.W. etc. Right-Step Clear Matte or Gloss Varnish

Surface

Wood memory album by Walnut Hollow

MERRY CHRISTMAS.

Just the same old Christmas greeting
Made dear by the days gone by,
With a wish we could be meeting
On this Christmas.—You and I

HEARTY
GREETI

color Mixes

Chair

Cobalt + Titanium White

+ Titanium White

Cobalt

+ Pure Black

Glow
Yellow Ochre + Titanium White

Yellow Light Glaze and Yellow Ochre Glaze

Apron & Tablecloth

Cobalt + Alizarin Crimson + Titanium White

+ Titanium White

+ Titanium White

Cobalt + Alizarin Crimson

Hair

Ice Blue

+ Burnt Sienna

Titanium White + Burnt Sienna + Ice Blue

Shirt
Red Light + Titanium White

+ Yellow Ochre

+ Burnt Sienna

+ Titanium White

Yellow Light + Titanium White

Flesh
Portrait

+ Raw Sienna + Burnt Sienna

Red Light + Yellow Ochre + Portrait

+ Burnt Sienna

Dress
Yellow Ochre

+ Raw Sienna

Yellow Ochre + Yellow Light + Titanium White

Pants & Fire

Red Light + Yellow Light

+ Yellow Light

Red Light

+ Pure Black

THIS PATTERN may be hand-traced or photocopied for personal use only. Enlarge at 161 percent to bring it up to full size.

PREPARATION & BORDER

1 Sand the surface and seal with wood sealer. Let dry and sand again. Measure 1 inch (2.5cm) and 1¼ inches (3.2cm) around the outside of the album cover, leaving a ¼-inch (0.6cm) band on four sides, 1 inch (2.5cm) in from the edge. Mask the outside edges of this band with blue low-tack masking tape. Apply three coats of Pure Gold Metallic acrylic. Let dry.

Mask the outside edge of this border with another layer of the blue masking tape; cover the hinges with masking tape for protection. Base the outside border with Raw Sienna.

In the photo below, the base colors appear without the tape around the borders.

2 With the gold borders masked off, begin to layer colors for the leather texture. First, tap a dry sea sponge into Pure Gold Metallic acrylic, tap the sponge on the palette to evenly distribute the color, then apply to the surface. Twist and turn the sponge for an irregular pattern. Let some of the Raw Sienna background show through. Wet the sponge and add a second sponged layer, this time with Burnt Umber, letting the gold show through. The thinned paint will create softer, more uneven textures on the gold background.

3 Repeat with additional layers of Pure Gold Metallic and Burnt Umber until you achieve the leathery effect desired. Add more Burnt Umber to the outside edges for an antiqued look. The more layers you apply, the more texture you will achieve. Eventually it will even have the feeling of leather.

SANTA & MRS. CLAUS

4 Transfer the pattern to the surface using transfer paper and a stylus.

Mix Cobalt and Titanium White, then basecoat the chair. Base the suspenders and the pants with Red Light. Mix Titanium White, Cobalt and a touch of Alizarin Crimson to make a light mauve, then basecoat the apron and the tablecloth. Mix a medium gray using Pure Black and Titanium White to base in the boots. With Titanium White, base the hair, apron trim, book and cuffs of pants. Base the flesh with Portrait.

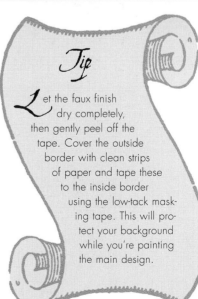

Tip

Let the faux finish dry completely, then gently peel off the tape. Cover the outside border with clean strips of paper and tape these to the inside border using the low-tack masking tape. This will protect your background while you're painting the main design.

5 Brush-mix Titanium White and a touch of Red Light for a light pink. With this color, base the left side of the shirt, which will be in shadow. Add some Yellow Ochre to the pink mixture and indicate the folds in the shirt, as a value between the shadow and the highlight.

Brush-mix Titanium White and a touch of Yellow Ochre to base in the glowing light portions of the shirt, dress, floor, faces and hands. Paint the shadows of Mrs. Claus's dress with Yellow Ochre.

6 Lighten the light details of the apron by adding Titanium White to the previous mauve mixture. Add a touch more Alizarin Crimson to the mixture for the darker values.

Paint a few highlights on the upper arms of the chair with a lighter mixture of Titanium White added to the base color. Add Pure Black and more Cobalt to the base color to paint the shadows around the left shadow side of the chair. Paint the chair's darkest shadows with Pure Black. Add Pure Black crease-shadows to the boots.

7 Brush-mix some shadow flesh colors using combinations of Raw Sienna, Burnt Sienna and Portrait. Add the necessary darker values to shade the eyes, nose, cheeks, hands and around the eyeballs of both figures. Overlap the values for softness by mixing a series of flesh-color values and dry-brushing the edges.

8 Add more details to the facial features with dark mixes made by adding Burnt Sienna and Burnt Umber to Portrait. Darken the shadows under the eyelids and inside the mouth, and base the irises of the eyes. Mix values of Red Light, Yellow Ochre, Portrait and Titanium White and paint lighter values on the faces and hands. With a mix of Titanium White and a touch of Yellow Ochre paint the highlights. The sides of the faces and hands by the fireplace should be more yellow.

HAIR

9 Paint the shadow-side waves of the hair, beard, mustache and eyebrows with Ice Blue. Add a touch of Burnt Sienna to the Ice Blue for additional shadow details. This will give a warm glow to the shadow areas. Make a mixture of Titanium White, a touch of Burnt Sienna and a smaller touch of Ice Blue, and use this soft, warm white in the highlight areas.

10 Add more glow to the hair with a thin glaze each of Yellow Light and Yellow Ochre mixed with blending gel. Glaze the mixtures over the right side of the hair, faces and hands.

For the shadow side, mix Ice Blue and a touch of Cobalt with blending gel for a cool glaze. Add this to the shadow areas for touches of cool shadows on the hair, faces and hands.

Base the pipe with a series of grays made from Pure Black and Titanium White, then add Pure Black accents.

SANTA'S SHIRT & PANTS

11 Add Burnt Sienna to the mix of Titanium White, Red Light and Yellow Ochre (used in step 5) and paint additional details on the shirt shadows and directly under the left arm down to the waist. Add this shadow under the right arm as well. Lighten this mixture with a touch of Titanium White, thin with blending gel, then tap in some texture in the middle areas of the shirt. Add more highlights to the upper-right portions of the shirt with a mixture of Titanium White and Yellow Light. Add more shadows under the arm with Burnt Sienna.

12 Darken the shadow creases and undersides of the legs with Napthol Crimson. Add more light values to the tops of the pants with mixtures of Yellow Light and Red Light. Add more Yellow Light for the front highlights on the knees. Darken the deepest shadows with Pure Black.

Stroke a few light texture lines on the front of the suspenders with the same values used for the pants.

FUR & BOOTS

13 Mix light and dark value combinations of Ice Blue and a touch of Pure Black. Using the tip of the filbert brush, tap in the texture of the fur around the boots. Soften the edges with lighter values of this gray mixture. Leave the top right side quite light, then add a Burnt Sienna glaze over this light area for a warm glow.

For the boots, base the soles with Burnt Sienna, then add a light edge with Yellow Ochre. Add more Pure Black in the deepest shadows and for accent details.

DRESS

14 Mix Yellow Ochre and Raw Sienna and paint the darkest shadows. Add the middle tones with a mix of Yellow Ochre, Yellow Light and Titanium White. Add more Titanium White to this mixture for the highlights.

For the book, mix a series of light, middle and shadow grays with Titanium White and Pure Black to paint the details.

APRON & CHAIR

15 Brush-mix Cobalt, Alizarin Crimson and Titanium White for the middle-value mauve color of the apron. Add more Cobalt and Alizarin Crimson to this mixture for the shadows. Add more Titanium White for the highlights. Then add even more Titanium White for the highlights of the frills on top of the shoulder.

Add more shadows to the chair with Cobalt and Pure Black.

TABLECLOTH & TEDDY BEAR

16 Base the bear, floor, chair tassels and cookies with a mixture of Raw Sienna and Titanium White. Base the vest and buttons with a mixture of Red Light and Titanium White. Brush-mix values of gray with Titanium White and Pure Black for the mug and plate.

17 Add more shadows to the mug and plate by adding more Pure Black to the gray mix. Paint highlights with lighter grays. Add highlights to the tablecloth with the mauve mixture plus more Titanium White.

Add shadows to the tassel and the teddy bear with Raw Sienna. Base the bear's face with a mixture of Raw Sienna and Titanium White; add highlights to the tassel and the bear's body with this same mix.

18 Add Burnt Sienna shadows to the bear, cookies and tassel. Soften the edges of the fur texture with a mixture of Raw Sienna and Burnt Sienna, then add more shadows to the bear with Burnt Umber. Add shadows to the vest and buttons with Red Light.

Extend the cast shadow on the floor under the teddy bear with Burnt Sienna, then darken closer to the bear with Burnt Umber. Extend the shadow in front of the bear as well.

19 Add Pure Black details to the bear's face. Add Pure Black shadows around the chair and under the legs of the table. Add more highlights and shadows to the tablecloth using lighter and darker mixtures of the base color.

GIFT BOXES AND LOGS

20 Base the box with a blue mixture of Cobalt, Titanium White and Alizarin Crimson. Darken the shadow side of the box by adding a touch of Pure Black to the mix. Add more Alizarin Crimson to the base color for the ribbon.

Base the floor by the fire with a mixture of Yellow Ochre and Titanium White. Add Raw Sienna and gradually darken the floor down toward the box. Base the ends of the logs and the drum bands with a mix of Raw Sienna and Titanium White. Use a mix of Cerulean Blue and Titanium White for the drum's sides.

21 Shade the ribbon with a darker mixture of Cobalt, Alizarin Crimson and a touch of Pure Black.

Add shadows to the floor near the logs, drum and box with Raw Sienna. Then, directly under these items, add the darker portion of the cast shadow with Pure Black.

Darken the center area of the drum bands with Raw Sienna.

22 Add shadows to the center of the drum with Cerulean Blue. Add more shadows and highlights to the ribbon and the box. Note how the front edge of the box is darkest next to the light edge and lightest next to the dark edge. This dramatizes the values, giving the illusion of depth to the box sides.

Add shadows to the drum with more Raw Sienna, then add the darkest shadow with Burnt Sienna. Add texture to the logs with Burnt Sienna, then add more shadows with Burnt Umber. Add more Burnt Sienna to the floor cast shadows, then more Burnt Umber directly under the logs, box and drum.

23 Add the final details to and sharpen edges of the drum sides, box and ribbon.

FIREPLACE

24 Base the flames, tops of the logs and the floor with Yellow Light. Base the inside rocks of the fireplace and the bottoms of the logs with Raw Sienna. For the front rocks of the fireplace, mix Titanium White and Pure Black to make a medium gray value, then add Cobalt to make a soft blue-gray base color.

25 Add a little Red Light to the Yellow Light, for an orange, and paint the upper portions of the flames. Curve the strokes down into the yellow and around the outsides of the flames. Tap orange on the tops of the logs for bright glowing texture. Shade the logs and the edges of the inside rocks with Burnt Sienna.

Base one stocking with a mix of Cobalt, Alizarin Crimson and a touch of Pure Black. Base the other with a mix of Alizarin Crimson, Titanium White and a touch of Pure Black.

26 Add Pure Orange to the lower edges of the front divider spaces between the rocks.

For the stockings, mix darker and lighter values of the previous mixtures. Tap darker texture around the outside edges and lighter-value texture in the center portions of the stockings. This will add roundness and dimension to the stockings.

FINISHING TOUCHES

27 Fill in the shadow inside the fireplace, the metal grate holding the logs, the details under the logs and the details of the rocks on the front of the fireplace with Pure Black. Add detail to the rocks with a mixture of the original blue-gray lightened with Ice Blue.

Base the colored ornaments with reds, oranges, yellows and blues. Lighten each color with Titanium White for highlights on the lower right portion of each ball. Add Pure Black to each of the colors to add darker shadows to the upper left portion of each ornament.

Paint in the candy canes on the tree and the candlesticks on the mantle. Base the back wall with a deep blue-gray mixture similar to the base color for the fireplace rocks.

Base the tree and the mantle foliage with Hauser Green Medium. Add the dark shadows with Hauser Green Dark and Pure Black. Add a few highlights to the front tips of the pine needles with Yellow Ochre.

To protect the album after the surface is completely dry, add multiple coats of either matte or gloss varnish. You will need at least three or four coats for full protection.

Busy Elves

THE JOLLY OLD ELVES ARE BUSY PLANNING, DIRECTING AND HELPING each other paint a tree design on the den wall. Of course the younger elf is the one who has to climb the ladder and paint the top decorations, while being assisted by his willing helper holding the bucket of paint up to his reach. A third relaxing elf has just mixed the next fresh batch of red paint for the young artist, while the other old elf still insists that his plans and instructions on the scroll are the best and should be followed. Sound familiar?

The two side panels are groups of toys, gift boxes and alphabet blocks that are fun additions. Each of the designs could be painted on many other surfaces, either together or as separate units.

Materials

Paints

FolkArt Artists' Pigment Acrylics: Burnt Sienna • Burnt Umber • Cerulean Blue • Cobalt • Hauser Green Dark • Hauser Green Light • Hauser Green Medium • Ice Blue • Medium Yellow • Portrait • Pure Black • Raw Sienna • Raw Umber • Red Light • Sap Green • Titanium White • Yellow Ochre

FolkArt Acrylics: Butter Pecan

Brushes

Royal Fusion: 3130 no. 6 flat or 3170 filbert • 3250 no. 3 round • 3585 no. 2 script liner

Royal Regis: 405 no. 6 bristle fan

Additional Supplies

sandpaper • J.W. etc. First-Step Wood Sealer • FolkArt Glazing Medium • graining comb • sea sponge • tracing paper • white transfer paper • stylus • FolkArt Blending Gel Medium • J.W. etc. Right-Step Clear Matte or Gloss Varnish

Surface

Wood fireplace screen by Wood Creations

color Mixes

Face & Hands

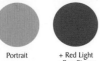

Portrait   + Red Light + Raw Sienna   Portrait + Red Light + Yellow Ochre   Titanium White + Red Light + Yellow Ochre

Hair & Apron

Yellow Ochre   + Titanium White   Raw Sienna   + Titanium White   Burnt Sienna

Beard, Bells & Paint Can

Pure Black   + Titanium White   + Titanium White

Pants

Cerulean Blue   + Titanium White   Cerulean Blue + Pure Black   Cobalt   + Titanium White   Cobalt + Pure Black

Paint

Red Light   + Medium Yellow   Red Light + Burnt Sienna   + Pure Black

THESE PATTERNS may be hand-traced or photocopied for personal use only. Enlarge the pattern above first at 200 percent then at 125 percent to bring it up to full size. Enlarge the two patterns at left first at 200 percent then at 152 percent to bring up to full size.

SURFACE PREPARATION & FAUX FINISH

1 Sand and seal the surface with wood sealer. If the grain rises, lightly sand the surface again. Base the entire surface with Titanium White. Let this completely dry.

Create a mix of Raw Sienna and glaze medium, mixed 2:1. The glaze medium will slow down the drying time, allowing you to move the paint around when making the wood grain. Using the bristle fan brush, apply vertical strokes of this mixture over the surface. Hold the brush at about a 45° angle and let the strokes show.

2 While the surface is still wet, drag the graining comb down the length of the surface to begin the graining texture. Slightly overlap each of the previous graining strokes.

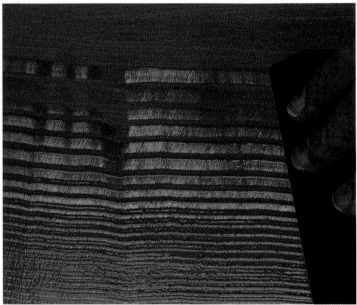

3 Soften the grain strokes by lightly dragging the fan brush down the length of the grain. Hold the brush by the end of the handle, so you don't apply pressure to the brush. The bristles should touch just enough to soften the edges of the grain. Let this layer completely dry.

4 Mix another glaze, this time using Raw Umber and glazing medium, mixed 2:1. Apply this glaze over the grain with the fan brush. Use long vertical strokes and add multiple layers until the desired grain is achieved (when the final varnish is applied, these wood grain colors will darken slightly). Let this layer completely dry.

5 Mix a glaze of Butter Pecan and glazing medium, mixed 2:1. Apply this glaze over the surface with the fan brush. Use long vertical strokes and add multiple layers until the desired grain is achieved. Let this layer completely dry.

6 Dampen the sea sponge and tap it into Burnt Umber. Continue to tap the sponge on your palette to remove any excess paint and to evenly disperse the color in the sponge. Gently tap the sponge around the outside edges of the panels to give them an antiqued look. Twist and turn the sponge as you apply the color to make an uneven, non-repeating pattern. Let this completely dry. The entire board now has an overall wood-grain pattern with darker antique edges.

ELVES ↑→

There are four elves at work painting and decorating the Christmas tree. I will show you painting steps for two of the elves. The other two are painted with the same mixtures and steps.

7 Position the pattern on the surface then tape the top outside corners of the pattern for stability. Position white transfer paper under the pattern and trace the design using a stylus. Base the faces and hands with Portrait.

8 Brush-mix a shadow color using Portrait, Red Light and Raw Sienna. Apply this paint to the shadow areas of the faces and hands. Keep the paint relatively dry when applying, then soften the edges with a mixture of values in between the shadow mix and Portrait. This stage is just blocking in the mass areas of shadows; no details are added yet.

9 With Burnt Umber, apply the deep shadow details at the hairline, around the eyebrows, inside the ears, under the nose, under the chin and around the eyes. Soften the shadow edges with washes of Burnt Sienna.

10 Brush-mix a medium blue using Cerulean Blue and Titanium White to fill in the iris of the eyes. Use a mix of Ice Blue and Titanium White to paint in the eyeballs. Mix a blush color for the cheeks, the lips and inside the ears with a mixture of Portrait and Red Light.

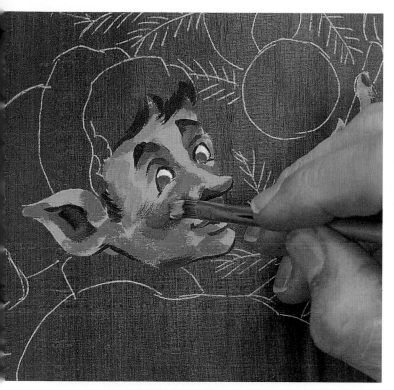

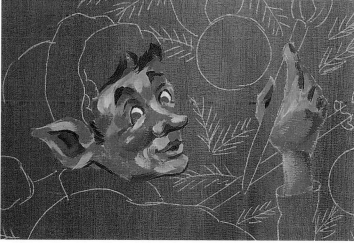

11 Add more lights to the faces and hands by mixing Portrait, Red Light and Yellow Ochre for softer middle values. Overlap this mixture with the previous darker values to soften the edges. Mix a lighter flesh value using Titanium White, Red Light and Yellow Ochre. Overlap the previous darker values. For the highlights, add more Titanium White to the previous mix. Stroke these brighter colors in the faces and hands, leaving the texture of the brushstrokes. These strokes and textured value changes will add action and character to the figures.

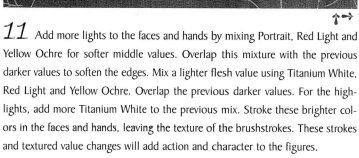

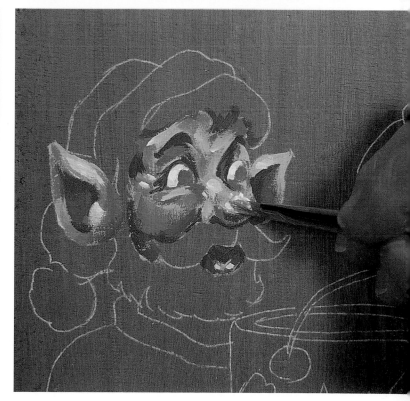

12 Add Pure Black outline details under the chin and ear, around the eyes and inside the mouth; fill in the pupils of the eyes as well. Add a sparkle to the eyes with a small Titanium White dot touching the iris and the pupil.

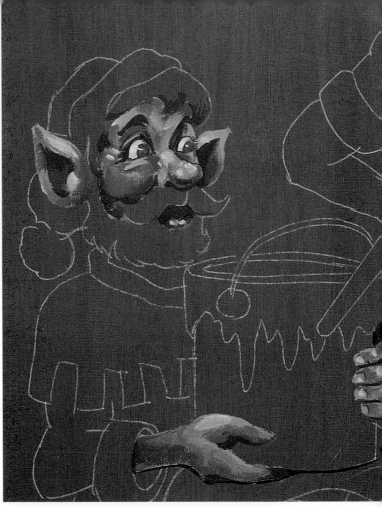

ELVES' CLOTHES

13 Using Yellow Ochre, base in the hair, hat fur, shirt and apron of the young elf. Add shadows with Raw Sienna to the bottom areas of the hair and hat fur, under the shirt collar, under the arms and in the apron. Most of the apron is in shadow, so make it slightly darker overall.

14 On this elf, use Yellow Ochre to base the hat, collar and shoulder, shirt cuff, apron and shoes. Shade the undersides of these areas with Raw Sienna.

15 Brush-mix in-between values of Yellow Ochre and Raw Sienna to soften edges between the values. Continue to add more lights with mixtures of Titanium White and Yellow Ochre.

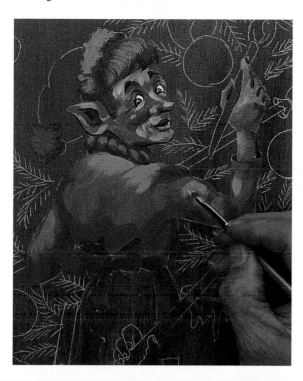

16 Soften the edges with in-between values. Use the same light mixtures as in step 15 for this elf's hat, shoulder and cuff.

←↑
17 Add Titanium White highlights to the tops of the shoulders, hats, sleeves and the first elf's hair. Add more details and shadows to the aprons with Burnt Sienna, then add darker shadows with Burnt Umber. Paint the final detail accent shadows with Pure Black.

18 For the pants and hat of the first elf and for the jacket and hat rim of second elf, mix a light value mix of Cerulean Blue and Titanium White. Base these areas with a light value, and then add more Titanium White for the highlights. Overlap the shadows with darker values of Cerulean Blue, then add the darkest accent shadows with Pure Black.

On the second elf, base the leotards with Cobalt, then add highlights with a mix of Cobalt and Titanium White. Add shadows to the outside edges of the legs with a mix of Cobalt and Pure Black. Base the bands with Red Light, then add shadows to the outside edges with a mix of Red Light and a touch of Pure Black.

20 Using the no. 3 round or the liner brush, add highlights with Titanium White. Add a few darker shadow accents with Pure Black.

BEARD & MUSTACHE

19 Mix a medium/light gray with Titanium White and Pure Black. Comb in the shadow of the beard, mustache and hair. Add more Titanium White for the lighter gray areas at the front of the beard.

PAINT CAN

22 Base the paint can with a light gray mixture of Titanium White and Pure Black. To make the shine on the metal can, paint vertical strokes of lighter gray values. Base the handle with light gray, then add the highlight on the top edge with Titanium White

SHOES

21 Add more dark shadows to the leotards with a glaze of Pure Black. Using a gray mix of Titanium White and Pure Black, base in the bells on the shoes. Add Titanium White highlights, then add the final details with Pure Black.

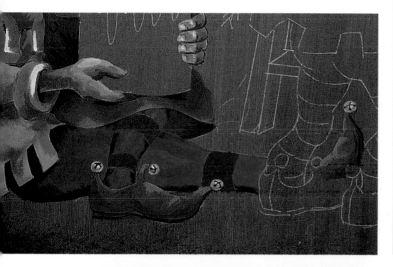

23 Add more darks to make the metal can shine. Mix darker values by adding more Pure Black to the original mix.

24 Base the spilled paint at the top of the can with Red Light. Add Medium Yellow to make an orange for the highlights on the top of the can and on the upper left portions of the paint drips.

The other paint cans are painted the same way. For the blue can, mix values with Cobalt, Titanium White and Pure Black; for the yellow can, use values of Medium Yellow, Yellow Ochre, Raw Sienna and Titanium White.

PAINT CAN, CONTINUED

25 Darken the shadows of the paint drips by mixing a small amount of Burnt Sienna into the Red Light. Make a darker value by adding a small amount of Pure Black to this mixture for the shadows inside the can and under the paint drips on the side of the can. Detail the handle of the can with Pure Black.

PINE NEEDLES

26 Reinforce the original tracing of the pine needles using the no. 3 round brush and Hauser Green Medium. Pull one stroke for the stem of the branch, then pull each needle from the outside to the main stem.

27 Fill in the darker shadows around and between the branches with Hauser Green Dark. Fill in more shadows around the ornaments and on the undersides of the larger branches in the center of the tree with Hauser Green Dark and a touch of Pure Black.

28 With the no. 3 round brush and Pure Black paint, place the shadow details of the pine needles on the inside branches and at the base of the outside branches. This will add depth to the branches going inside the tree. Continue to add details to the smaller branch stems and needles with Pure Black.

29 Highlight a few of the outside branches with Hauser Green Light on the round brush. Pull the strokes from the outside tips of the needles in toward the center of the branch.

30 Brush-mix a medium blue with Titanium White and Cobalt, and base in the ornament and the brush. Add more Cobalt for shadows on the outside edges of the ornament and the details in the brush. Base in the red ornament with a mix of Red Light and Titanium White. Add more Red Light for shadows on the outside edges of the ornament.

31 Add Titanium White for the highlights to the red and blue ornaments and the brush. Add darker shadows with straight Red Light and Cobalt to make the ornaments round and to add more details to the brush. Shade the underside of the brush with Pure Black.

32 Load the no. 3 round brush with a healthy amount of Titanium White paint, making sure to have the brush tip full of paint. Make the chain of beads in curved rows looping from branch to branch by simply tapping down on the surface using the same pressure for each tap so each bead is the same size.

MIDDLE PANEL

33 To finish this panel, base the shadows of the ladder with Burnt Sienna; create the wood grain with Burnt Umber. Paint the light side of the ladder with a mix of Raw Sienna and Titanium White; add highlights with this mix plus more Titanium White. Use these same values to paint the elf's pole.

Base the angel with Portrait, then add light and dark flesh values as described in project three. Create the hair's golden tones with values of Medium Yellow, Yellow Ochre and Raw Sienna. Paint the wings with values of Ice Blue, Titanium White and Burnt Umber.

Follow the instructions in project one for painting the holly leaves and berries.

35 Add more Titanium White to the Yellow Ochre mix for an off-white to fill in the very top panels of each box.

Add Titanium White to the Raw Sienna and stroke in the reflected lights and highlights on the ribbon.

Add more Titanium White to Raw Umber for a lighter value and stroke in the reflected lights on the shadow sides of the boxes. Overlap the shadow areas of the dog to fill in the middle values of his body.

Mix a light blue using Cerulean Blue and Titanium White to base in the rocking horse. Then add more Titanium White for a lighter value and add in the highlights.

Base in the teddy bear with a mixture of Titanium White and Burnt Sienna.

LEFT SIDE PANEL

34 Base the light sides of the boxes with a light mixture of Titanium White and Yellow Ochre. Base the ribbons with Raw Sienna. Base the shadow sides of the boxes with a light mixture of Titanium White and Raw Umber. Loosely fill in only the shadow areas of the dog with this same mixture.

Titanium White + Yellow Ochre

Titanium White + Raw Umber

Titanium White + Yellow Ochre

Titanium White + Burnt Sienna

Two values of Cerulean Blue + Titanium White

Two values of Raw Umber + Titanium White

36 Using a mix of Titanium White and Yellow Ochre, stroke in the highlights on the front sides of the boxes, concentrating on the front edges closest to the shadow edges.

With a mix of Raw Sienna and a touch of Burnt Sienna, paint the shadows of the ribbons, under the bow and on the front edges of each box closest to the highlight edges.

Using a mix of Raw Umber and Titanium White, stroke in the shadows on the shadow sides of the boxes, concentrating on the front edges of each box closest to the highlight edges.

Mix a very light warm gray for the dog highlights using Titanium White and a touch of Raw Umber. Then add the highlight details with Titanium White.

Add shadow details to the horse with Cerulean Blue values, overlapping the previous lighter values.

Mix lighter and darker values of Titanium White and Burnt Sienna for the bear details, tapping in the values for texture with the no. 3 round.

Base the top ribbon with a mix of Titanium White, Cerulean Blue and a touch of Yellow Ochre for a light muted green. Add highlights with mixes of the base color and Titanium White; add shadows with mixes of the base color and Pure Black.

Base the remaining ribbons with Red Light, and then add the highlights with a mix of Red Light and Titanium White. Add shadows with a mix of Red Light and a touch of Pure Black.

Titanium White + Yellow Ochre

Two values of Burnt Sienna + Titanium White and straight Burnt Sienna

Two values of Cerulean Blue + Titanium White

Cerulean Blue

Raw Umber and two values of Raw Umber + Titanium White

37 Add the final details to this panel. Sharpen edges with light or dark colors as needed, and add Pure Black shadow outlines and Titanium White highlights.

Follow the instructions in project one for painting the holly leaves and berries.

RIGHT SIDE PANEL

38 Base the rims on the light side of the blocks with a mix of Yellow Ochre and Titanium White.

With Yellow Ochre, base the front side of the blocks around the letters, most of the letters on the shadow side and the trim on the soldier.

Base the shadow side of the blocks with a mix of Titanium White and Raw Umber for a light warm gray. Brush in only the shadows of the cat with this same mix.

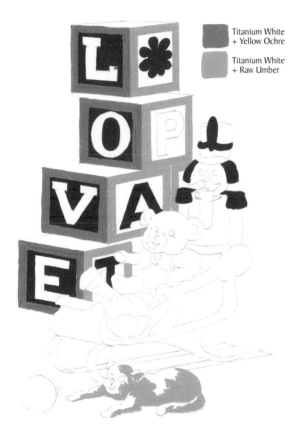

Titanium White + Yellow Ochre

Titanium White + Raw Umber

39 Mix a warm off-white using Titanium White and Yellow Ochre and fill in the very top panels of the blocks.

Mix a light gray value using Titanium White and Raw Umber to stroke in the reflected lights on the shadow sides of the blocks. Fill in the middle value areas of the cat with this same mix.

Mix a light value of Cerulean Blue and Titanium White to base in the uniform of the soldier and the runners of the sleigh. Add more Titanium White for the highlights.

Mix a dark green with Sap Green and a touch of Titanium White to base in the sleigh, then add more Titanium White for the highlights.

Mix a light value with Burnt Sienna and a touch of Titanium White and base in the bear. Add more Titanium White for the highlights and more Burnt Sienna for the shadows.

Mix Titanium White and Yellow Ochre to add some highlights to the soldier's uniform trim and to the flower on the top block.

Titanium White + Yellow Ochre

Titanium White + Burnt Sienna and straight Burnt Sienna

Two values of Titanium White + Cerulean Blue

Two values of Sap Green + Titanium White

Two values of Titanium White + Raw Umber

Titanium White + Yellow Ochre

Two values of Titanium White + Burnt Sienna and straight Burnt Sienna

Two values of Titanium White + Cerulean Blue and straight Cerulean Blue

Three values of Titanium White + Raw Umber

40 Using a mix of Titanium White and Yellow Ochre, stroke in the highlights on the rims on the front of the blocks, concentrating on the front edges of each box closest to the shadow edges.

With a mix of Raw Umber and Titanium White, stroke in the shadows on the front sides of the blocks, concentrating on the front edges of each block closest to the highlight edges.

Using a mix of Raw Sienna and a touch of Burnt Sienna, stroke in the wood grain of the blocks on the front side. Base the shadow side of the blocks and the inside panel of the sleigh with Burnt Sienna, then add wood grain with Burnt Umber.

Mix a very light warm gray for the cat highlights using Titanium White and a touch of Raw Umber. Add highlight details with Titanium White.

Add more shadow details to the soldier with Cerulean Blue values, overlapping the previous lighter values.

Add more details to the sleigh with lighter values of Sap Green and Titanium White.

Mix lighter values of Titanium White and Burnt Sienna for the bear details, tapping in the values for a fur texture.

Base the remaining letters, bow, ball and yarn with Red Light, then add the highlights with a mix of Red Light and Titanium White. Add shadows with a mix of Red Light and a touch of Pure Black.

→

41 Add the final details to this panel. Sharpen edges with light or dark colors as needed, and add Pure Black shadow outlines and Titanium White highlights.

Follow the instructions in project one for painting the holly leaves and berries.

42 To finish this project, varnish with either matte or gloss varnish.

Santa & Teddy Bear

THIS CLASSIC SANTA COULD BE PAINTED IN EITHER OILS OR ACRYLICS. For this particular design, I prefer oils because they help me to achieve the softer edges around Santa. It's also easier to create additional depth around the figure, making the center of interest Santa's face as he admires his toy teddy bear.

Materials

Paints

Permalba Oils by Martin/ F. Weber Co.: Alizarin Crimson • Burnt Sienna • Burnt Umber • Cadmium Red Light • Cadmium Yellow Light • Cadmium Yellow Medium • Cobalt Blue Genuine • Ivory Black • Paynes Gray • Raw Sienna • Raw Umber • Sap Green • Phthalo Green • Titanium White • Yellow Ochre

Prima Oils by Martin/ F. Weber Co.: Cerulean Blue

Prima Acrylic by Martin/ F. Weber Co.: Iridescent Gold • Ivory Black • Titanium White

Brushes

Royal Fusion: 3130 no. 6 flat or 3170 filbert • 3250 no. 3 round • 3585 no. 2 script liner

Additional Supplies

sandpaper • J.W. etc. First-Step Wood Sealer • tracing paper • gray and white transfer paper • stylus • RapiDry Oil Medium • Turpenoid or Turpenoid Natural • sea sponge • J. W. etc. Right-Step Clear Matte or Gloss Varnish

Surface

Wood Platter by Multi-Ply Wood Design, Inc.

color Mixes

Teddy Bear

Raw Umber

+ Titanium White

+ Titanium White

Hair

Paynes Gray + Titanium White

+ Yellow Ochre

+ Burnt Sienna

Tree

Phthalo Green + Ivory Black

+ Titanium White

+ Yellow Ochre

Berries & Coat

Cadmium Red Light + Alizarin Crimson

Alizarin Crimson + Ivory Black

Cadmium Red Light + Cadmium Yellow Medium

Flesh Colors

1. Raw Sienna + Cadmium Red Light

+ Titanium White

+ Titanium White

2. Burnt Sienna + Titanium White

+ Titanium White

3. Yellow Ochre

+ Titanium White

4. Alizarin Crimson + Sap Green + Cadmium Yellow Medium

+ Cadmium Yellow Medium

For this project I've premixed a series of basic flesh colors, and I refer to them by number in the instructions. Mix these colors on your palette in a straight line directly under the parent color.

1. Medium value: Raw Sienna + Cadmium Red Light. Pick up a portion of this mixture and place it directly under the original mix. Add a small amount of Titanium White. Take a portion of this mixture and add another small amount of Titanium White.

2. Light value: Burnt Sienna and Titanium White

3. Light value: Yellow Ochre and Titanium White

4. Shadow value: Alizarin Crimson and a touch of Sap Green and Cadmium Yellow Medium. Pick up a portion of this mixture and place it directly under the original mix and add more Cadmium Yellow Medium.

THIS PATTERN may be hand-traced or photocopied for personal use only. Enlarge at 200 percent to bring it up to full size.

SURFACE PREPARATION

1 Sand the surface until smooth. Seal the wood with wood sealer—this will slightly raise the wood grain. Sand the surface again. Basecoat the surface with Titanium White acrylic paint.

Position the pattern on the plate; slide the gray transfer paper under the pattern and trace Santa and the toys with a stylus. The pattern for the tree branches will be traced after the background is basecoated.

Fill in the entire background with a thin coat of Ivory Black acrylic, leaving all the edges soft. Around the fur, hair and beard, stroke from the outside in toward the image and lift the brush away from the surface to create a soft, irregular dry-brush effect. Around the remainder of the image, keep the edges soft; around the bottom keep it soft and random. It is better to apply two thin layers of color than to apply one thick layer—a thick layer will only leave undesirable ridges in the paint.

When this paint is dry, reposition the pattern on the surface and trace the tree branches using white transfer paper so the design will show on the black surface.

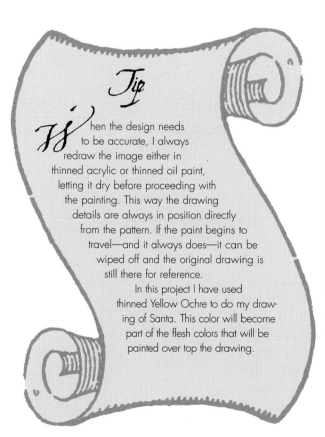

Tip

When the design needs to be accurate, I always redraw the image either in thinned acrylic or thinned oil paint, letting it dry before proceeding with the painting. This way the drawing details are always in position directly from the pattern. If the paint begins to travel—and it always does—it can be wiped off and the original drawing is still there for reference.

In this project I have used thinned Yellow Ochre to do my drawing of Santa. This color will become part of the flesh colors that will be painted over top the drawing.

PATTERN

2 Using a script liner brush, reinforce the pattern drawing with Yellow Ochre thinned with RapiDry Oil Medium.

FACE

3 Thin some Yellow Ochre with oil painting medium. Begin to block in the shadow areas of the face and beard using a no. 6 flat brush.

4 With a thin mixture of Titanium White and a touch of Paynes Gray, begin to add middle and shadow values to the hair and the outside edge of the beard.

With a mix of Raw Sienna, Cadmium Red Light and Titanium White (value 1), block in the shadows of the face. Add more Titanium White to this mixture for the middle values, and then add more Titanium White for the highlights. Using the no. 3 round brush, add the accent darker shadows with Raw Umber.

5 Darken the shadows of the face with Burnt Sienna. With the value 1 mixture of Raw Sienna, Cadmium Red Light and Titanium White, paint in the medium value details. Add more Titanium White to this mixture for the highlights. With a mix of Yellow Ochre and Titanium White (value 3), add more highlights. Add more Cadmium Red Light to the medium mixture to redden the cheeks and lips.

Accent the shadows in the hair and beard with more Paynes Gray and Titanium White, for a blue-gray.

EYES

6 Base the iris with Cobalt Blue Genuine. Add Titanium White to the Cobalt Blue Genuine for the lower half of the iris. Outline the iris with a thin line of Paynes Gray. Fill in the eyeball with a light mixture of Titanium White, Paynes Gray and Burnt Umber, using a slightly darker mix under the eyelid shadow and a lighter mix on the bottom half of the eyeball.

With values I and 4, add more shadow flesh to the right side of the forehead, around the eye socket and on the right side of the nose under the eyebrow. Soften these shadow edges with slightly lighter values.

FACE, CONTINUED

8 With the dark shadow color (value 4), darken the creases on the right temple and along the side of the nose. Soften the edges with the next lighter color. Add the medium value (value I) around the forehead and eyelids.

7 With Paynes Gray, base in the pupil and the shadow under the upper eyelid directly above the pupil. Continue the shadow under the upper eyelids with the darkest flesh color (value 4). Place a sparkle dot of Titanium White at the ten o'clock position, touching the pupil and iris. With a lighter value of Cobalt Blue Genuine and Titanium White, place a reflective light at the four o'clock position.

9 Continue to add more lights to the forehead with value I. Add medium highlights with the value 2 mix to the eyelids, bridge of the nose, below the eyebrows, under the eye, between the eyebrows and forehead. Add dark shadow flesh to the balls of the cheeks and under the nose.

FACE, CONTINUED

10 Add Cadmium Red Light for blush to the lower balls of the cheeks and to the corners of the lips. Add darker warm shadows using a mixture of the value I mix and Cadmium Red Light to define the nose shadow, cheeks and tongue. Shade the lips with the darkest middle value and highlight with Titanium White.

Use the value 4 shadow color to place a small shadow under the mustache, around the ball of the nose and to make the laugh lines around the eyes.

BEARD & HAIR

11 Mix Paynes Gray and Titanium White to paint the shadows around the waves of the hair and beard. Add more Titanium White to this mix for the middle-value areas.

12 Add more color to the shadows of the beard with a soft green mixture of Paynes Gray, Titanium White and Yellow Ochre. Using a no. 3 round brush, add this color as an accent to some of the shadows.

13 As you work toward the center of the beard, begin to lighten the values with more Titanium White and a tiny touch of Burnt Sienna added to the previous green mixture. Overlap the previous values for soft edges. Begin closing in on the highlight areas with lighter colors, continuing to leave the direct highlights as the white base color. Paint in the shadows of the lightest beard shapes with a warm mixture of Titanium White and a touch of Burnt Sienna, then paint in the highlights with straight Titanium White.

14 Thin Titanium White with plenty of medium and, using the script liner, add individual hairs in loose, long flowing strokes. Only a small number of detail lines are really necessary—just enough to create the illusion of detail. Less is better.

Because the paint is still wet, the white paint for the details will pick up some warm colors and some cool color. Let these new mixtures become the unity of the beard details.

HANDS

15 As with the face, begin by drawing the fingers with thinned Yellow Ochre using a liner brush.

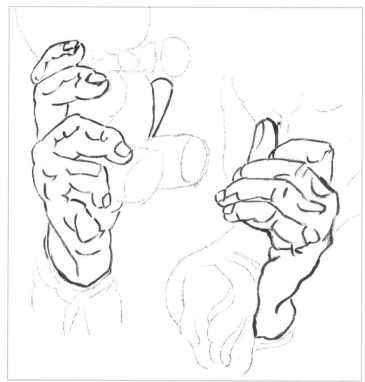

16 Thin the Yellow Ochre with oil painting medium and fill in the shadow areas only. Leave all the light areas as white surface.

17 With the same mixtures previously used for the face, apply deeper shadows with the darker mix under and between the fingers and on the wrists. Soften the edges with the next lighter value of flesh color.

18 With the lighter flesh values, fill in the light areas on the wrists and on the tops of the fingers, then add a lighter highlight value on top of the knuckles.

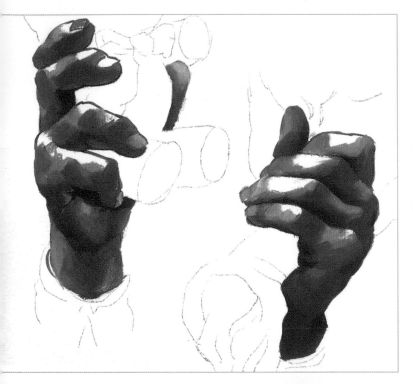

TREE

19 Load the round brush with a mixture of dark green made with Phthalo Green, Ivory Black and a touch of Titanium White, and stroke in the needles from the outside of each branch curving in toward the center stem.

20 Add a bit more Titanium White to the mix for a lighter value, and stroke more needles from the outside ends of each branch. This will fill in the ends of each branch for a fuller-looking tree.

21 Add a touch of Yellow Ochre to the previous mixture for a slightly lighter yellow-green and highlight the outer tips of the front branches only.

HAT & FUR

22 Base the hat and the berries with Cadmium Red Light.

Mix a light gray with Titanium White, Paynes Gray and Burnt Umber. Tap in the shadow areas of the fur and base the entire tassel with this light gray, then add darker shadows by adding more Paynes Gray to the mix. Pull a soft stroke over the background for a soft fuzzy edge. See project two for detailed instructions for painting fur.

23 Add more Paynes Gray to the previous mixture for a slightly darker value, and stroke in more shadows close to the underside of the holly leaves and the underside of the tassel and the waves of the hair.

24 Add shadows to the hat and berries with a mixture of Cadmium Red Light and Alizarin Crimson, then add a touch of Ivory Black for the darkest value. Add Titanium White to the mix for the highlights. See project one for details on painting leaves and berries.

Add more Titanium White to the Paynes Gray mixture to make some lighter values, then begin to add highlights to the fur and hair. Pull short fan-shaped strokes in each layer to create the soft texture of fur.

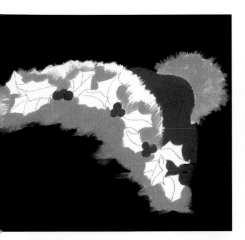

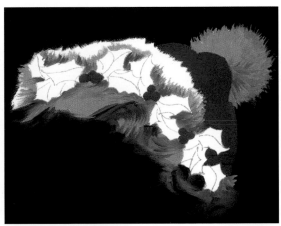

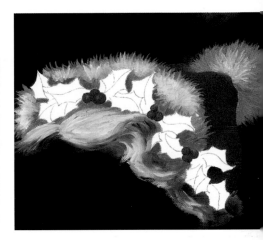

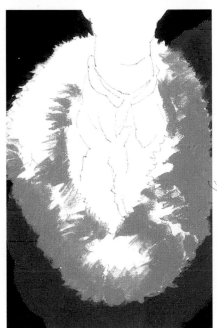

26 As with the hat, add darker values in the shadows of the fur cuff with more Paynes Gray. Keep the outside edges that overlap the coat and the background soft.

Paint the shadows of the coat with Alizarin Crimson.

COAT & CUFF

25 Base the coat with Cadmium Red Light. Mix Titanium White with a touch of Burnt Umber and Paynes Gray for a medium-neutral gray, then base in the shadows of the fur cuff.

COAT & CUFF, CONTINUED

27 Continue to darken the shadows of the coat with Alizarin Crimson, then add a touch of Ivory Black for a darker value in the deepest shadows. Add highlights to the coat by lightening the Cadmium Red Light with a bit of Cadmium Yellow Medium.

Add more Titanium White to the Paynes Gray mix and add these lighter values of gray to the fur cuff. Place the lightest values in the upper areas and toward the center of the cuffs.

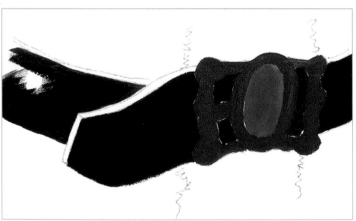

BELT

28 Base the belt with Ivory Black. Base the buckle with Yellow Ochre. Base the center stone with a medium blue mixture of Cobalt Blue Genuine and Titanium White.

29 Add lights to the belt with gray mixtures made from Titanium White and Ivory Black. The lightest part of the belt will be the top edge, on the curves closest to the light source.

On the belt buckle, add shadows with Raw Sienna and highlights with Yellow Ochre plus Titanium White. For the light and dark values on the center blue stone, add Titanium White and Ivory Black to the base color.

TEDDY BEAR

30 Reinforce the drawing with a mix of Raw Umber and Titanium White. Most of the teddy bear is painted with values of Raw Umber and Titanium White, for a soft yellow/gray, so the drawing will blend in with the painting.

31 Fill in the shadows with a medium value mix, then add darker values to the deep shadows. Tap in the color with the no. 3 round to give it a soft fuzzy texture.

32 Gradually add more Titanium White, tapping in each layer of color and making them lighter toward the top and center highlight areas. Base the shadows of the bow tie with Cobalt Blue Genuine.

33 With mostly Titanium White and a touch of Raw Umber, add highlights to the top of the head and on the face. Paint the little nose with a light pink. Mix Cobalt Blue Genuine with a touch of Titanium White and highlight the bow tie.

34 To keep the toys in the background, paint them with colors that are slightly grayer and more muted than the colors used on Santa or the teddy bear. I suggest adding a touch of Ivory Black to each color, or add the complementary color to each, to soften and tone down the colors. Even the highlights will be slightly darker in value.

Base the horse and gift box with values of Cobalt Blue Genuine; base the ribbon and candy cane stripes with a light gray mixture of Titanium White and Ivory Black.

Base the soldier's decorations and the horn with Yellow Ochre.

Fill in the shadows of the toy bag with Burnt Umber, blending the outside edges into the black background.

35 Add some of the light and dark flesh colors to the soldier's face. Paint in some darker shadows on the horn with Raw Sienna and middle values on the toy bag with Burnt Sienna.

36 Paint the candy cane stripes and the soldier's suit with values of Cadmium Red Light. Fill in the soldier's hat, eyes and mustache with Ivory Black and with grays made from Ivory Black and Titanium White.

Fill in the ball with values of Yellow Ochre and Raw Sienna. Highlight the toy bag with Raw Sienna, then a few brighter highlights with Raw Sienna and a touch of Titanium White. See the image at right for the completed toys and toy bag.

37 With a soft sea sponge, tap Iridescent Gold around the outside rim of the plate.

Coat the entire surface with a thin layer of RapiDry Oil Medium. This will seal the surface until the paint is dried and cured enough for the final varnish.

After at least two months of curing, apply a number of coats of gloss varnish, allowing the varnish to dry between coats.

Santa with Pipe

THIS CLASSIC PORTRAIT OF SANTA IS PAINTED IN ACRYLICS AND OILS using a technique similar to that used by the Old Masters. The subject is first painted only in gray values, that is lights and darks, which is called the "grisaille" (gray values). Then the painting is completed in color. This is a very accurate, controlled method and is especially useful when applied to portraits. Of course, this procedure can be used for any subject on any surface. Painting the grisaille will help you achieve a much more accurate and solidly based painting. And even though you will be painting the same picture twice, the finished piece will be completed much faster than you would think. I really believe you will immediately see the advantages and you will be amazed with your results.

Materials

Paints

Permalba Oils by Martin/ F. Weber: Alizarin Crimson • Burnt Sienna • Burnt Umber • Cadmium Red Light • Cadmium Yellow Light • Cerulean Blue • Cobalt Blue Genuine • Ivory Black • Raw Sienna • Phthalo Green • Titanium White • Yellow Ochre
Prima Acrylic by Martin/ F. Weber: Burnt Umber • Ivory Black • Titanium White

Brushes

(Two sets of brushes, one for acrylics and one for oils)
Royal Fusion: 3130 no. 6 flat or 3170 filbert • 3130 no. 1 and 12 flat • 3170 no. 8 filbert • 3250 no. 3 round • 3585 no. 2 script liner

Royal Regis: 405 no. 3 bristle fan
Royal Supreme White Bristle: 1AB no. 5 bright • 1AT no. 5 filbert

Additional Supplies

gesso or pretinted gray gesso • gray transfer paper • stylus • RapiDry Oil Medium • Turpenoid or Turpenoid Natural • J.W. etc. Right-Step Clear Matte or Gloss Varnish

Surface

16" x 20" canvas by Fredrix

THIS PATTERN may be hand-traced or photocopied for personal use only. Enlarge at 200 percent to bring it up to full size.

color Mixes

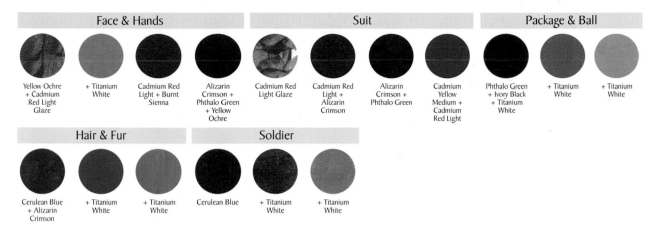

Face & Hands

Yellow Ochre + Cadmium Red Light Glaze	+ Titanium White	Cadmium Red Light + Burnt Sienna	Alizarin Crimson + Phthalo Green + Yellow Ochre

Suit

Cadmium Red Light Glaze	Cadmium Red Light + Alizarin Crimson	Alizarin Crimson + Phthalo Green	Cadmium Yellow Medium + Cadmium Red Light

Package & Ball

Phthalo Green + Ivory Black + Titanium White	+ Titanium White	+ Titanium White

Hair & Fur

Cerulean Blue + Alizarin Crimson	+ Titanium White	+ Titanium White

Soldier

Cerulean Blue	+ Titanium White	+ Titanium White

SURFACE PREPARATION

1 When I create an underpainting value study, I prefer to use a tinted canvas surface to help the placement of the values. By using a value close to value 5, all my middle values are already in place. Then I simply need to add my light values, then my dark values. It really simplifies the process of correct value placement.

So, to begin this project, cover the surface of the canvas with a pretinted gray gesso. If tinted gesso is not available, add a small amount of Ivory Black acrylic paint to some white gesso and mix thoroughly to get close to a value 5, then apply this to the canvas.

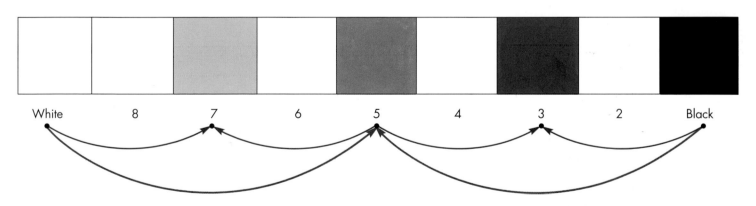

White   8   7   6   5   4   3   2   Black

TO MAKE A GRAY VALUE SCALE, begin with straight white and black paint. Place these colors on opposite ends of the scale. Then mix white and black in equal proportions to get a middle-value gray; place this color in the value 5 position. Mix white and value 5 to make value 7; mix black and value 5 to make value 3.

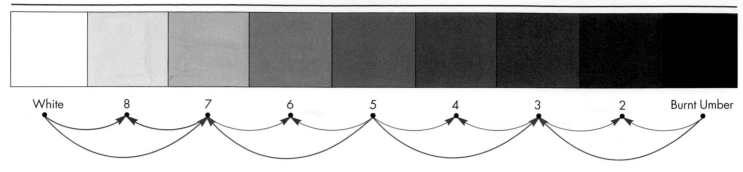

White   8   7   6   5   4   3   2   Burnt Umber

FOR THE GRISAILLE PAINTING, prepare another value scale on your palette with Titanium White and Burnt Umber acrylic paints as the end values. Mix the intermediate values, following the arrows above. The step-by-step instructions that follow refer to the values by number, so you may want to write the numbers on your palette or keep this diagram handy as you paint.

FACE, BEARD & HAIR

2 Transfer the pattern to the surface with gray transfer paper and a stylus. With a no. 3 round brush reinforce the pattern with highlights of Titanium White and shadows with a value 5 mix of Titanium White and Burnt Umber. By redrawing the pattern like this you will establish a balance of lights and darks in your drawing.

3 Since your canvas is already based with the value 5 tone, most of your middle values are already established. So now, with a no. 8 filbert brush, begin to mass in the larger areas of light with Titanium White.

4 The advantage of using the acrylics for the underpainting is the rapid drying time. This enables you to paint up and down the value scale, from dark to light and from light to dark, without creating mud. I have found that it is much easier to begin working the lighter values first. Therefore, add more of the details to the hat, face and beard areas with values 5 through 7.

5 When all the light values are in place it becomes very easy to begin applying the darker values, those in the value 3 range. Add the darker values, overlapping the previous strokes for soft value gradations, to form more roundness and depth around the eyes, cheeks and shadow of the nose.

6 Fill in the background with straight Burnt Umber. With slightly dry paint, soften the edges of the fur and hair with values 1 and 3; the dry-brush strokes will help to make a very soft, feathered edge. The soft edges will give you better gradations of values. Refine the light and dark values by adding more details.

HANDS

7 Using the same steps as used previously for the face, redraw the hands using a no. 3 round brush. Fill in the highlights with Titanium White and the shadows with a value 5 mix of Burnt Umber and Titanium White.

8 Add the lighter to middle values, those in the 7 range, around the fingers and hands. The base color of the canvas is your middle value (value 5).

9 Add slightly darker values to the shadow sides of the fingers. These values will be darker than the base color of the canvas.

10 With Burnt Umber, add the darkest values to the background and the darkest accent areas. Sharpen the edges around the hands, pipe and toy bag. These areas are intended to come forward; therefore they will have sharper edges. All areas that recede into the background will have softer edges.

TOYS & TOY BAG

11 As before, reinforce the drawing of the toys and toy bag with Titanium White for the highlights and a value 5 mix of Burnt Umber and Titanium White for the shadows.

12 The toys and bag are to be kept in the background, so most of the objects will be dark values, creating depth. There are very few highlights; in fact, the lightest values will be values 7 or 8. Use these values and a no. 8 filbert brush to mass in the light areas of the toys.

13 Add the darker values, values 5 and 7. Note that these are the same values that were used for the foreground areas, not darker. To make elements recede, make only the light areas darker (not the dark areas darker).

14 With straight Burnt Umber and value 3, paint in the darkest values and fill in the remainder of the background.

15 Paint in the values of the coat the same way as described for the other elements. The more detail and the more value changes you add at this stage, the easier it will be to apply the color overpainting.

16 Now, a series of thin oil color glazes will be applied over the grisaille to establish the color scheme. Then thicker, more opaque color will be added, using the underpainted values as a guide as to how light or dark to mix the color.

17 Using the no. 3 bristle brush, apply a very thin coat of RapiDry Oil Medium over the entire canvas. This will allow your brush to glide over the surface as you paint the oil color wet-into-wet.

Brush-mix a thin glaze of Yellow Ochre and Cadmium Red Light and RapiDry. Apply this wash over the entire face to begin creating a color scheme for the flesh colors. You will see that even with this first glaze of color, the underpainted values create the form.

18 Add a touch of Titanium White to the previous mix to make the paint more opaque. Mix the colors to the same values as the underpainting. Using a no. 5 bright or filbert brush, begin to apply the more solid color values over their counterparts in the underpainting. You will gradually convert the gray underpainting values to color.

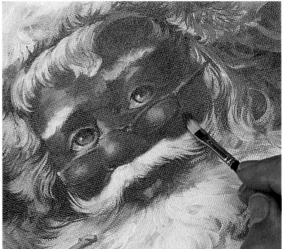

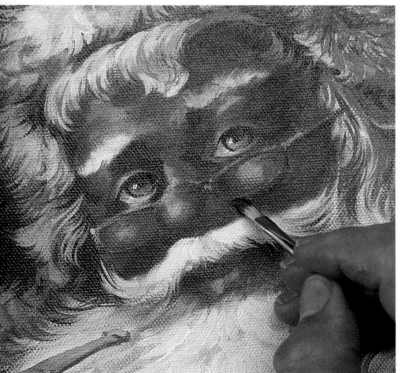

19 Add a thin layer of Burnt Sienna over the shadows, still letting some of the underpainting show through in these dark areas. For the mouth and cheeks, add some Cadmium Red Light to the Burnt Sienna.

20 Apply Burnt Umber to the darkest shadow areas, softening the edges into the Burnt Sienna shadows. Using a small round or a script liner, brush-mix a small amount of Alizarin Crimson, Phthalo Green and Cadmium Yellow Medium and add the deepest shadow accents and crevices of the creases around the eyelids and inside the nostrils and mouth.

EYES

21 Brush-mix Cerulean Blue and Titanium White for the irises. The values should already be in the underpainting, so all you need is a wash of color. Mix a medium gray from Titanium White and Ivory Black for the eyeball, painting it darker at the top, under the eyelid, and lighter toward the bottom of the eyeball.

22 Paint the pupils with Ivory Black using the liner brush. Lighten the lower left side of the iris with a lighter mix of Cerulean Blue and Titanium White. With straight Titanium White, add the tiny highlight spot touching the iris and the pupil at the one o'clock position.

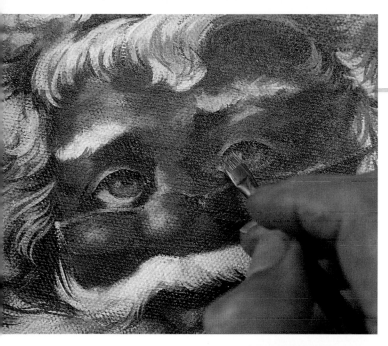

FACE HIGHLIGHTS

23 Mix a highlight flesh color using Titanium White, Yellow Ochre and a tiny touch of Cadmium Red Light. Lighten the forehead, between the eyebrows, down the front of the nose, on the top of the cheeks, on tops of the eyelids and on the front of the mouth.

EYEGLASSES

24 Base the frames with Raw Sienna. Add the shadows under the frames with Burnt Sienna. Add lights with Yellow Ochre; add the highlights with a mix of Yellow Ochre and Titanium White. Paint on a few little sparkle highlights of straight Titanium White, and you have bright gold eyeglasses.

HANDS & PIPE

25 Dampen the hand area with a thin layer of oil medium. Paint the hands with a transparent glaze of Yellow Ochre and Cadmium Red Light using a no. 8 filbert brush. Add more Cadmium Red Light to the mix and paint the middle and dark areas of the hands.

27 Add highlights to the top portion of the fingers and the knuckles with a light mixture of Titanium White, Yellow Ochre and a touch of Cadmium Red Light. Add slightly more Titanium White to the mix for the lightest areas of the front knuckles.

26 Add Burnt Sienna to the previous mixture and apply the darker shadows of the hand and the pipe with a no. I flat brush. Again note that the roundness created by the underpainting values of the pipe are still showing through when the thinned Burnt Sienna is applied. No additional color mixing is necessary.

PIPE DETAILS

28 With a mixture of Cadmium Yellow Medium and Yellow Ochre, fill in the band and the stem of the pipe. Highlight these areas with a mix of Titanium White and Yellow Ochre to give the appearance of a brighter, lighter gold.

Using the tip of the no. 3 round brush, tap in Cadmium Red Light for the embers in the barrel of the pipe. Add Ivory Black for the ashes, painting them darkest in the outer corners inside the bowl. With Ivory Black, outline the detail of the shaft and the top portion of the barrel and create the deepest shadows of the pipe.

SANTA'S SUIT →

29 With a large soft brush, apply a thin layer of oil medium over the entire coat area. Mix a glaze of Cadmium Red Light and more oil medium and paint a thin layer over the entire coat and hat area, then add drier paint to the middle and light areas. You want this color to be much more brilliant than the flesh areas, therefore you need to apply slightly thicker layers than those first glazes used for the flesh. To glaze with Cadmium Red Light, an opaque color to begin with, you will need to spread the paint out evenly over all the values to blend them.

With Alizarin Crimson mixed with the Cadmium Red Light, begin to darken the shadows in the folds and under the arm on the back of the coat.

30 Deepen the darkest shadows with more Alizarin Crimson. For the deepest shadows, darken the Alizarin Crimson with a touch of Phthalo Green for a very deep burgundy.

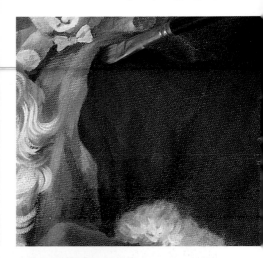

31 Apply additional layers of Cadmium Red Light and Alizarin Crimson to the middle and light areas. Tap the brush on the surface to create some texture. Additional Cadmium Red Light layers will brighten and deepen the color.

32 Highlight the tops of the folds with a red-orange mix of Cadmium Yellow Medium and Cadmium Red Light.

Tip

B oth Cadmium Red Light and Alizarin Crimson are very slow-drying colors. So let these paints set up for a short period of time before applying additional layers for deeper, richer reds. If they are too wet when you apply additional layers, you may experience some lifting of color.

SANTA WITH PIPE

119

BACKGROUND & SMOKE →

33 Base the entire background with Ivory Black. Work the background paint right up to the figure so that everything that's painted from this point forward can be painted over the background for a soft edge. When the background is dry, paint in the smoke by loading the no. 6 flat brush with a very thin transparent wash of oil medium and Titanium White. Holding the brush at an angle, lightly touch the surface, then pull just the corner of the brush in wiggly strokes across the surface. This will make wispy strokes of smoke.

TOYS & TOY BAG

34 Apply a thin base color over the toy bag with Burnt Sienna and Burnt Umber. Add more Burnt Umber to the darkest shadows and under the bag so the edge blends into the black background.

Brush-mix Alizarin Crimson and Cobalt Blue Genuine to base the purple package behind the toys. Mix a touch of Phthalo Green, Ivory Black and Titanium White and base in the left package.

35 With a mixture of Ivory Black and Phthalo Green, paint in the small tree with short strokes. Keep the shadows dark, then paint the highlights with the previous mixture plus a touch of Cadmium Yellow Medium.

For the tree ribbon, mix Titanium White, Cerulean Blue and Alizarin Crimson for the base color, then add more Titanium White for the highlights. Base the package bow with Alizarin Crimson, then add Titanium White for the highlights.

36 With Cobalt Blue Genuine and Titanium White, mix various values of lights and darks for the soldier's suit and hat. Lighten this color with more Titanium White, then add a touch of Alizarin Crimson to make a light blue-gray and paint the middle values on the airplane. Add Ivory Black for the shadow values, blending the edges. Add details to the windows of the airplane with Ivory Black.

Finish the front folds of the toy bag with Raw Sienna, and highlight with Yellow Ochre.

37 With Burnt Sienna make short straight strokes for the lion's mane. With Burnt Umber add some darker strokes to the mane and detail the eyes, ears and mouth. Using short tapping strokes, base the lion's body with Raw Sienna. Highlight the eyes, mouth and ears with Yellow Ochre. Add lighter highlights with a mix of Yellow Ochre and Titanium White.

Base the soldier's uniform details with Yellow Ochre. Add the brightest highlights with a mix of Yellow Ochre and Titanium White. Mix Titanium White, Yellow Ochre and Cadmium Red Light for the flesh. Add more Titanium White for the highlights. Detail the face and uniform with Ivory Black.

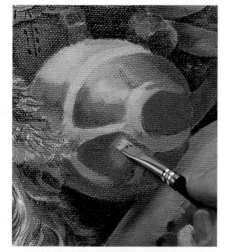

BALL

38 Begin painting the ball with the darkest values, making values of Phthalo Green and a touch of Ivory Black (adding Titanium White to lighten as needed) to match the underpainting. Even though the design pattern of the ball is light, values that are light and dark, relative to each other, are still needed to give the ball its shape and roundness.

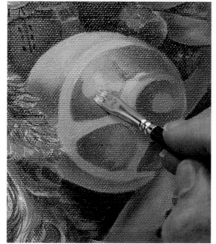

39 Add more Titanium White to the mixture for the lightest values on the top center of the ball.

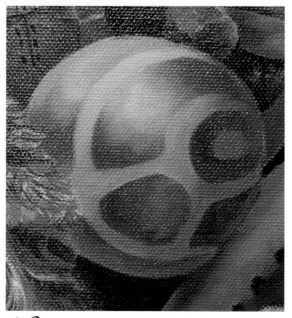

40 For the brightest highlight, add more Titanium White.

DRUM

41 Use the middle value of the ball mix to paint the side panel of the drum. Paint Burnt Sienna in the darkest shadows of the drum rim. Add Raw Sienna for the middle value and Yellow Ochre for the lightest value. Highlight the top rim with a mixture of Titanium White and Cadmium Yellow Medium.

Use a brush-mix of Ivory Black and Titanium White on the script liner to draw the string detail on the side of the drum and the deepest shadow on the inside of the rim.

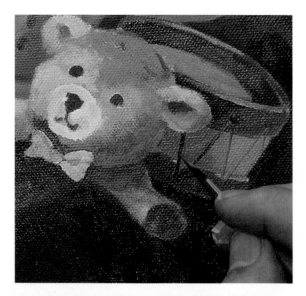

TEDDY BEAR

42 Matching the values of the underpainting, mix Burnt Umber and a touch of Titanium White for the dark shadows. Tap in the color to create the fur texture. As you work toward the lighter values, add Raw Sienna for the middle values, then add Titanium White to the mixture for the lighter values.

BELT & BELLY AREA

44 Paint the darkest areas of the belt buckle and buttons with Burnt Sienna. Add darker accent shadows with Burnt Umber on the bottom edges of the buttons and the upper left corner of the buckle.

43 Mix Titanium White and Yellow Ochre for the lightest highlights on top of the bear's nose, above the eyes, and on the chin and front ends of the arms.

Mix Alizarin Crimson and Titanium White for the bear's bow tie; add more Alizarin Crimson for the shadows and more Titanium White for the highlights. With Ivory Black, finish the facial details and add shadows where the bear is in front of the drum. Use Titanium White to add a few highlights to the nose, chin and above the eyes.

45 Fill in the middle values of the buckle and buttons with Raw Sienna.

Highlight the belt with a dark gray mix of Ivory Black and Titanium White. The top edges of the belt will be slightly lighter to give thickness to the belt. Highlight the very top front tip of the belt to give the appearance of it projecting forward.

46 Add Ivory Black shadows around the belt buckle. Use the Ivory Black and Titanium White mix to make gradations of value on the buckle edges and in the center of the buckle area.

Mix Titanium White and Yellow Ochre for the brightest highlights on the belt buckle. The very front edge of the buckle should be the lightest and have the sharpest edge.

HAIR, BEARD & FUR

47 Using a no. 12 flat brush apply glazes of Cerulean Blue and Alizarin Crimson over the darker shadows of the beard to soften the outside edges. The lower portions away from the light source should be darker; the outside edges overlapping the garment should be softer. You want these areas to recede so the highlights can come forward, creating the third dimension.

Tip

Most of the values of the beard and fur are already in place with the acrylics. The next stage is to begin adding hue and intensity of colors with glazes of color to the shadows. Even though the beard is to appear white, the shadows need to be cooler colors; the lights need to be warmer colors. Make the glazes by loading a brush with RapiDry Oil Medium and then adding small amounts of color. In this case a combination of Cerulean Blue and Alizarin Crimson.

By adding layers of glazes, we give the painting more depth. The glazes cause the light rays to bend and bounce through each layer of transparent color before it reflects back to our eye. The vibration of depth is created by the light rays bending as they travel into the painting and then bouncing as they come back out.

HAIR, BEARD & FUR, CONTINUED

48 On the fur cuff, begin with the same glazes on the outside edges, and then add Titanium White to the glaze to make it more opaque. Using the chisel edge of the brush, paint short fan-shaped strokes, pulling out from each center. Overlap each lighter value as you work your way into the center of the cuffs. The hair is done the same way, only using much longer, wavy strokes.

49 Continue to add the light purple glaze to all the shadow areas on the hair, hat, cuffs and coat center panel.

50 Mix a warmer glaze with a brush-load of oil medium and a touch of Burnt Sienna. Apply this glaze to the middle and light value areas of the beard, hair and fur.

51 Go back to the mix of Alizarin Crimson and Cerulean Blue and add more Titanium White to stroke in some additional details in the shadow areas. Again, make short straight strokes for the fur and long wavy strokes for the hair.

52 With Titanium White and Burnt Sienna, begin to close in a little bit toward the highlight areas, overlapping the shadow areas. Continue the same strokes, short for the fur and long for the hair.

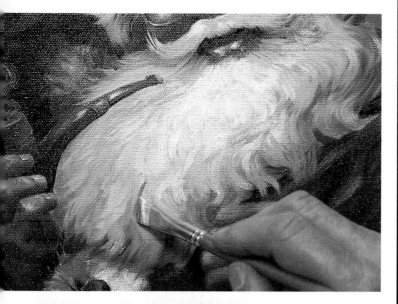

54 Using the script liner and thinned Titanium White, add the individual hair details to the eyebrows, mustache, tufts of hair and brim of the hat and cuffs. Keep the pure white details toward the center areas so they remain the focal areas with the brightest highlights. Add a few details around the outside area with Titanium White grayed slightly so it's not as bright.

53 Continue with this mix until you have completed the warm highlights in the beard, hair and fur.

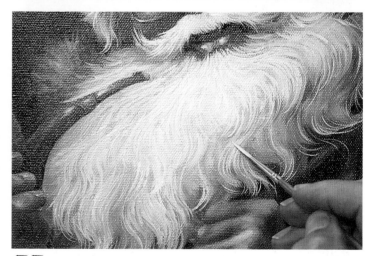

55 Continue the same process, using long flowing strokes for the beard. Add the whitest details to the top areas of the waves. This will be the first area that the viewer will see and adding even a few hairs will give the illusion of a lot of detail. Refer back to page 115 for the finished painting.

Seal the painting with a thin layer of RapiDry Oil Medium. This will protect the painting until it has had time to cure. Then, after at least two to six months, apply a final varnish, gloss or matte. I prefer gloss varnish on an oil painting.

RESOURCES

Surfaces

BENT OAK FARM
9511 Woodland Way
King George, VA 22485
(540) 775-2407

CHRISTMAS BY KREBS CO.
3911 S. Main St.
P. O. Box 5730
Roswell, NM 88201
(505) 624-2882
www.christmasbykrebs.com

MULTI-PLY WOOD DESIGN, INC.
46 Grey Street
Fredericton NB, Canada E3B 1V7
(800) 550-2325

PORCELAIN TREASURES
3446 McCutcheon Road
Columbus, Ohio 43219
(614) 471-7407

TARA MATERIALS, INC.
111 Fredrix Alley
Lawrenceville, GA 30046

WALNUT HOLLOW
1409 State Road 23
Dodgeville, WI 53533
(800) 950-5101
www.walnuthollow.com

WAYNE'S WOODENWARE, INC.
1913 CTH II
Neenah, Wisconsin 54956
(800) 840-1497

WOOD CREATIONS
Tom Mingolello
Palm Harbor, Florida
(727) 785-6746

WOODCRAFTS
P.O. Box 78
Bicknell, Indiana 47512
(800) 733-4820

Paints

PLAID FOLKART
3225 Westech Dr.
Norcross, GA 30092
678-291-8100
(800) 842-4197
www.plaidonline.com

MARTIN/ F. WEBER CO.
2727 Southampton Rd.
Philadelphia, PA 19154
(215) 677-5600

Brushes

ROYAL BRUSH CO.
6707 Broadway
Merrillville, IN 46410
(800) 247-2211

Other Materials

J.W. ETC.
2205 First St., #103
Simi Valley, CA 93065
(805) 526-5066
www.jwetc.com

Canadian Retailers

CRAFTS CANADA
2745 29th St. N.E.
Calgary, ON, T1Y 7B5

FOLK ART ENTERPRISES
P.O. Box 1088
Ridgetown, ON, N0P 2C0
(888) 214-0062

MACPHERSON CRAFT WHOLESALE
83 Queen St. E.
P.O. Box 1870
St. Mary's, ON, N4X 1C2
(519) 284-1741

MAUREEN MCNAUGHTON ENTERPRISES
RR #2
Bellwood, ON, N0B 1J0
(519) 843-5648

MERCURY ART & CRAFT SUPERSHOP
332 Wellington St.
London, ON, N6C 4P7
(519) 434-1636

TOWN & COUNTRY FOLK ART SUPPLIES
93 Green Lane
Thornhill, ON, L3T 6K6
(905) 882-0199

INDEX

EXPLORE DECORATIVE PAINTING WITH NORTH LIGHT BOOKS!

LEARN TO PAINT MINIATURE decorative painting masterpieces with these 14 full-color, step-by-step projects, including Victorian vanity boxes, wooden nesting dolls, holiday ornaments and more.

All the instructions are supplemented with hints and sidebars, complete materials lists, color palettes and designs ready to be hand-traced or photocopied. A glossary of terms and techniques completes the package so that you'll never be without guidance.

0-89134-992-8, paperback, 128 pages

LET ELIZABETH HAYES, CDA help you harvest a bounty of fresh-picked fruit in your paintings, from blueberries and cherries to apples, bananas and melons. Her detailed, friendly instruction and twelve step-by-step projects will show you how to paint fruit that looks good enough to eat.

Whether you're a beginner or an experienced painter, you'll learn to fill your home with luscious, ripe fruit. The hardest thing will be selecting which project you'll start first.

1-58180-078-9, paperback, 128 pages

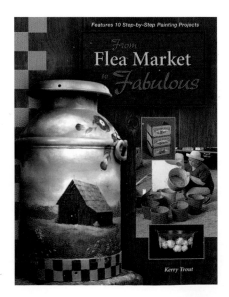

FANTASTIC TREASURES AWAIT YOU, hidden among piles of junk at garage sales and swap meets. With this book, you'll be able to transform these spectacular bargains into the kind of art and furniture you'd be proud to have in your home, plus you'll have a great time in the process!

In ten gorgeous step-by-step projects, author and artist Kerry Trout shows you how to choose flea market finds and turn them into fabulous family heirlooms.

1-58180-092-4, paperback, 144 pages